RAND

More Than 25 Million Acres? DoD As a Federal, Natural, and Cultural Resource Manager

David Rubenson, Marc Dean Millot, Gwen Farnsworth, Jerry Aroesty

Prepared for the
Office of the Secretary of Defense

**National Defense
Research Institute**

PREFACE

This report examines potential future directions for the Department of Defense's (DoD's) program for natural and cultural resource management of the 25 million acres of DoD federal land. More than just the land is at issue in this management. The report presents a briefing that emphasizes the implications of external trends in science, politics, societal values, and demographics for the resource management obligations of the DoD. The work was conducted within the Acquisition and Technology Policy Center of RAND's National Defense Research Institute, a federally funded research and development center sponsored by the Office of the Secretary of Defense, the Joint Staff, and the defense agencies. The work was conducted for the Deputy Under Secretary of Defense for Environmental Security.

In addition to those in the DoD, this report should interest environmental activists, federal land managers, and personnel in various other federal agencies.

CONTENTS

Preface   iii

Summary   vii

List of Acronyms and Abbreviations   xxiii

Chapter One
   THE BRIEFING   1
   Introduction   1
   Research Questions and Approach   3
      "More Than 25 Million Acres?"   3
      Approach.   5
   Overarching Laws and Policies.   19
   Agency-Specific Laws and Policies   21
      BLM and USFS.   21
      DoD   22
   Fort Bragg.   27
   The Military-Ecology-Legal Interaction   28
   A Fragile Program?   30
      The Transfer of Integrated Training Army
        Management, Program Rationales, and Core
        Values   30
      Funding and Personnel   31
   New Science, Policies, and Problems   36
      Conservation Biology   37
      Ecosystem Management   38
   Ecological Islands   41
   Conservation Biology, Legal Compliance, and the Military
      Mission   42

The Species-Area Curve   47
Application to a Military Base   48
The Requirements   50
The Constraints   51
Military Conservation Biology?   52
The Mojave Desert Ecosystem Management Initiative . . .   55
    Evolution of the Initiative   55
    Lessons for DoD Ecosystem Management   58
Camp Pendleton   60
Fort Bragg   61
Yakima   62
The Political Process for Extended Lands: Public
    Involvement   75
    Idaho and "Strange Bedfellows"   75
    A Special Constituency   77
The Political Process for Extended Lands: Detailed
    Legislation   79

Chapter Two
    CONCLUSIONS   109

SUMMARY

BACKGROUND

The late 1990s will be a critical period for the Department of Defense's (DoD's) environmental program.[1] The program has expanded rapidly in the last 10 years, and Congress is now examining virtually every aspect of DoD's environmental activities. The expansion was rooted in growing community concerns about hazardous waste pollution. By the mid-1980s, Congress mandated by law, and authorized budgets for, the DoD development of a program to address these problems.

The result of that initiative was rapid growth in the DoD's environmental program despite the shrinkage of the department's overall budget. From 1985 to 1995, the DoD's environmental program grew from less than $1 billion annually to more than $5 billion per year. Even prior to the 1994 congressional elections, there was a growing realization that the program had to move beyond its origins of hazardous waste emergency response toward solving DoD's long-term environmental challenges with greater efficiency and purpose.

This report focuses on one aspect of DoD's $5 billion per year environmental program, the roughly $200 million per year program to manage natural and cultural resources on its 25 million acres. Even

---

[1]When discussing the Department of Defense, we are including all DoD agencies and services. At times, we will specifically refer to the Army, Navy, Air Force, and Marines. We do not discuss the role of the Civil Works Division of the Army Corps of Engineers.

though this program element has not been the focus of DoD environmental program development, it has expanded in response to greater regulatory scrutiny of all DoD activities.

Several factors motivate special attention to this program element at this time. Natural and cultural resource management has a more direct impact on the military mission than any of the financially larger elements of DoD's environmental program. This small program element could easily be decimated if included as a part of a generalized downsizing. Even more important would be loss of the experience that has been gained in overcoming organizational and internal cultural problems to develop the current fragile program.

Perhaps most significant, a review is motivated by the contradictory and oscillatory external political forces guiding DoD's natural and cultural resource management requirements. Motivated partially by an emerging scientific consensus, the Clinton administration has embraced the conservation of biodiversity as a policy goal. The administration's policy instrument, ecosystem management, calls upon federal agencies to consider problems in the context of ecological rather than federal agency boundaries. Conversely, the new Congress is scrutinizing all DoD environmental expenditures and conducting a general review of natural resource law from a perspective that places greater emphasis on utilitarian and development values.

The question of necessity, appropriate design, and survivability of the DoD natural and cultural resource program is therefore raised, requiring an assessment of the program in light of recent and enduring developments. This report considers the role of the DoD's natural and cultural resource program by reviewing developments over the last 10 years and, more important, by identifying future challenges and their impact on program requirements.

STRUCTURE OF THE REPORT

The report is presented in its orginial briefing format.

We introduce the report by providing background on the DoD environmental program and the role of the natural and cultural resource management program element. We then discuss the origins of our effort to conduct the special examination mentioned above. Our approach was motivated by a question from a senior DoD policymaker regarding the nature of broad social, scientific, political, and ethical trends in American society that will affect DoD's natural and cultural resource management obligations.

At the time this approach was being formulated, the DoD was being encouraged to actively participate in the Clinton administration's policy of ecosystem management. This policy calls for federal agencies to look beyond the boundaries of their own lands and consider land management from an ecosystem perspective. This provides a significant challenge for DoD agencies, which focus on their military mission. As our research progressed, the 1994 elections sent distinctly different signals, perhaps suggesting that DoD could reduce its emphasis on natural resource management. Given these somewhat contradictory influences, we engaged in an iterative process and redefined the policy questions in the following manner:

1. What internal and external factors currently provide the motivation and political framework for DoD natural and cultural resource management?

2. What external trends may ultimately force DoD to develop a more outward-looking and broader orientation toward natural and cultural resource management?

3. What external trends may allow DoD to reduce its emphasis on natural and cultural resource management and how enduring are these trends?

4. How does DoD integrate countervailing external signals into an effective natural resource management program that reflects societal values and accounts for the need to maintain lands and waters for military training?

More generally we are asking whether or not DoD needs to consider the implications of resource management issues beyond the boundaries of its base and the criticality of doing so. Hence, the question, "*More Than 25 Million Acres?*" has both a literal and a figurative meaning.

We seek to answer the first policy question in the beginning of the report where we review the traditions, mechanisms of governance, problems, and changes that have characterized the DoD natural and cultural resource management program in the last 10–15 years. The report then highlights societal trends that may be motivating a broader DoD role, including DoD's involvement in issues beyond the boundaries of its bases. We explore how DoD may be affected by the habitat surrounding its bases and by the "extended lands" that DoD may seek to acquire, fly over, sail near, or use on a temporary basis. We also examine the potential impact of the 104th Congress and the external forces that may imply less-intensive DoD obligations. Finally, we summarize our findings and programmatic recommendations.

CURRENT MOTIVATIONS: THE DEPARTMENT OF DEFENSE AS FEDERAL LAND MANAGER

We review the role of DoD as a federal land manager, describe the factors motivating DoD interest in resource management, and compare that role to the role of large land management agencies. We note that DoD manages 25 million acres of federal land (of which technically 16 million acres is withdrawn public land[2]). DoD is a smaller federal land owner compared with the Department of Agriculture and the Department of Interior agencies, which together manage 650 million acres of federal land. However, DoD is the third-largest federal landholder in the United States, and its lands are ecologically significant, containing roughly as many distinct threatened and endangered species as the lands of any other land management agency.

This ecological richness raises the issue of balancing military needs and ecological values. We discuss the political process that guides DoD in achieving this balance. We note that DoD is subject to two distinct political processes: one for managing the military mission

---

[2]Withdrawn land was formerly available for public use, as is much of the roughly 300 million acres of public land managed by the Bureau of Land Management. Withdrawn land is land removed from the public domain that theoretically may still be returned for public use at a later date. Some withdrawal acts specify the return dates. Individual withdrawals of 5,000 acres or more must be approved by act of Congress.

and a different one for managing federal lands. The latter process is oriented toward the Department of Interior and Department of Agriculture, although DoD is still subject to the resulting "overarching" laws and policies, such as the Endangered Species Act (ESA), the National Environmental Policy Act (NEPA), and the Clinton administration's Ecosystem Management Initiative. However, DoD is subject to far less "agency-specific" legislation or public scrutiny on its 25 million acres than are the large land management agencies. Congress and the public provide detailed management oversight of the land management agencies but traditionally have tended to give DoD more discretion in its land management function.

Noting the different political governance, we compare one of the large land management agencies (the U.S. Forest Service) with the DoD in terms of organization, structure, and perspective. We observe that DoD's natural and cultural resource program is "inward looking," organized to support the military mission, and organized to comply with the overarching laws mentioned above. Its primary constituent is within the organization. Agencies like the U.S. Forest Service are organized to cope with external constituencies. Nevertheless, complying with overarching laws has proven to be a difficult task for DoD, especially when these laws have a direct impact on the ability to conduct the military mission. Although some of DoD's 25 million acres consist of buffer zones and unusable terrain, there is often a close interaction among legal compliance, conservation of ecological values, and ability to conduct the military mission. We describe the difficult and even painful steps DoD has had to undertake to build a fragile inward-looking program that copes with these diverse impacts. The complexity of organizational issues was recently highlighted by the Army's decision to transfer proponency for one of its most important resource management program elements, the Integrated Training Area Management program (ITAM), from the land managers to the combat training function.

We conclude by noting that within the DoD, two issues provide convincing rationale for the cultural and natural resources program: legal compliance and maintenance of the resources to support military training. However, the generalized nature of natural resource law and the complex legal-ecology-training interaction precludes a narrow interpretation of these core rationales. DoD should also be aware that the pursuit of other conservation goals may better connect the institution to core values in American society.

MOTIVATIONS FOR A BROADER ROLE?

We then analyze emerging factors that may challenge an inward-looking program. First—a recent outcome from the political process for managing federal lands and partly based on the emerging multidisciplinary science of conservation biology—is the Clinton administration's ecosystem management policy, which calls for a multi-agency approach and examination of ecological problems beyond an agency's boundaries. Our central question is whether DoD participation will support the core rationales of legal compliance and military training, or whether ecosystem management only enhances unrelated ecological values. Although DoD (at the policy level) has voiced its willingness to participate, the effectiveness and survivability of the initiatives within DoD will depend on the connectivity to legal compliance and military training.

Ecosystem Management and Conservation Biology

Before discussing ecosystem management, we provide a demographic backdrop to the discussion. We note that population growth has been highest in areas where DoD has significant numbers of installations, leaving many DoD installations as "ecological islands" and the subject of increased regulatory attention (in particular, from those responsible for enforcing the Endangered Species Act). We use Camp Pendleton as a case study to demonstrate the linkage between these "islands" and the difficulty of managing a base for both legal compliance and military training.

We then review some of the basic principles of the emerging science of conservation biology, which provides some of the motivation for the administration's ecosystem management policy. This science, which is still coalescing, aims to develop tools and models to help land managers conserve biodiversity in damaged and fragmented habitats. As such, its aims correspond closely to supporting DoD's challenge of managing "ecological islands." However, conservation biology seeks to conserve biodiversity, which is not always identical to achieving legal compliance.

Nevertheless, conservation biology's focus on ecological islands provides a scientific basis for evaluating significant aspects of DoD's land management problem. One of conservation biology's most significant relationships is the species-area relationship. This relationship implies that not only do "ecological islands" contain endangered ecology, but that the ecology is also more difficult to manage than when this land was part of a larger, healthier ecosystem. Conservation biology predicts that because of developments beyond base boundaries, resource management strategies once adequate on military bases could become obsolete, even if DoD has maintained its lands with consistency and care. Failure to adapt to these changes could lead to increased problems with regulators and natural resource law.

We discuss the implications for the current "inward-looking" program. We argue that the recently concluded multispecies endangered species consultation concluded between Camp Pendleton and the U.S. Fish and Wildlife Service may represent the kind of activity that moves the program toward the principles of conservation biology while maintaining the necessary priority for short-term legal compliance and military training–related requirements. We outline an approach that will help DoD develop a type of "military conservation biology" that reflects DoD's internal programmatic constraints and its role as a unique type of federal resource manager.

We then focus on the DoD participation in the regional habitat planning implied by conservation biology and ecosystem management policy. We argue that while regional habitat developments are a core DoD concern that can ultimately make legal compliance more difficult, selective engagement and thorough preparation is required for participation in regional habitat planning. We review several cases in which DoD installations have tried to engage in such planning, including the Mojave Desert Ecosystem Initiative. This case study leads us to conclude that in some situations, the costs of engagement outweigh the potential benefits. To determine when such circumstances exist, and to effectively engage when appropriate, the existing program will need significant improvements in its ability to understand, analyze, and participate in regional ecological processes and politics.

We conclude that although ecosystem management emerged from consideration of ecological values and the political process for managing federal lands, it can nonetheless support DoD core interests of compliance and mission viability. However, a blanket DoD policy to engage in regional ecosystem management is too coarse for the wide variations in the political and ecological conditions of highly diverse DoD installations. Additional planning and analysis capabilities are required to help determine when such engagement is desirable.

DoD Role in "Extended Lands"

We also review the DoD role on "extended lands" (the lands DoD flies over, sails near to, or seeks to acquire on a temporary or permanent basis). We note that although the Rocky Mountain West has undergone a significant percentage of population growth, it has had a small absolute growth, and much of that has occurred in urban centers. As a result, many large tracts of public land are still unoccupied, but there are an increasingly large number of locally and nationally organized groups laying claim to use of the land. In particular, there is a political synergy between the moral authority of Native American claims and the organizational capability of environmental groups.

The increased demand by various groups for use of undeveloped public land competes with the needs of a military mission requiring an expanded geographical range. DoD's need for new land will continue to grow with the deployment of new technologies and training approaches. We discuss this trend and provide two detailed examples. Although simulations and other options may at times offset the need for new land, the DoD has engaged in several new efforts to utilize off-base lands and to expand and rearrange airspace and land holdings.

Efforts to change boundaries (including new use of airspace), either temporarily or permanently, place DoD natural and cultural resource management in a vastly different political setting than that experienced within existing boundaries of bases. No longer is DoD subject solely to overarching laws with little outside security. Rather, new initiatives ignite the political process and make DoD subject to the same—if not more intense—legislative and public scrutiny as the land management agencies. This was dramatically and painfully demonstrated in the Air Force's recent decision to abandon—or at least drastically alter—plans to expand Mountain Home Air Force Base in Idaho. We recommend that the military services thoroughly exhaust all multiservice land and airspace use options and conduct a thorough military needs assessment before requesting any temporary or permanent change in boundaries.

We observe that the political process for managing federal lands has different implications for DoD depending on whether issues fall within "existing" or "changing" boundaries. DoD's current program is guided by an inward orientation, and we describe how DoD's failure to recognize this distinction has worked against it. The distinction is most critical for the Air Force, which because of the lack of a land mission has not had to face the legal-ecological-military interaction on its own bases. However, because of its airspace requirements, the Air Force has the greatest need to engage in issues beyond the boundaries of its own bases. We suggest that the forthcoming process to renew DoD's use of withdrawn public lands may well be governed by the "changing" boundaries process even though no boundaries need be altered.

Finally, we note that in activities involving changing boundaries, DoD is asking its natural resource program to go beyond the traditional support goals of legal compliance and training land conservation to help change and improve DoD's basing and training structure. To make such an adjustment in perspective and goals, the program inevitably requires additional support, resources, encouragement, greater access to information, and dialogue with other military functions.

THE NEW DEBATE: MOTIVATION FOR LESS-INTENSE MANAGEMENT?

We discuss the implications of the broad environmental review being undertaken by the 104th Congress. This review is being conducted from a utilitarian and development perspective and may suggest that DoD can reduce its commitment to natural resource protection.

Although it is still too early to determine if this represents an oscillation or a broad long-range shift in American environmental policy, it now appears that prior to the 1996 elections Congress may not make radical revisions to natural resource law in a way that affects DoD obligations. Current versions of new endangered species bills emphasize the rights of private property owners and do not specifically alter federal responsibilities, although change in species-listing procedures and changing emphasis in "burdens of proof" would have important long-term effects. The most significant near-term relaxation of requirements for DoD may be the result of reduced regulatory agency budgets for enforcement of overarching laws. However, such administrative measures are easily reversed.

We then examine the risks to DoD of falsely interpreting the debate as a fundamental change in national values and requirements. Of greatest risk may be the temptation to save funds by reducing the scope of the natural and cultural resource program, forcing DoD to relearn the painful organizational lessons of the past decade. We also point out that the current congressional debate seems to place significant emphasis on flexibility, potential exemption options, and use of cost-benefit analysis. To adapt to these changes, DoD may actually need to increase the breadth of its natural and cultural resource management program by acquiring new capabilities for strategic planning and analysis. This need may exist even if near-term political actions lead to less-intense management requirements.

Finally, we review a supporting RAND analysis of 25 years of serial opinion surveys on political attitudes toward wildlife. These data indicate that Americans have slowly but steadily adopted a greater interest in the aesthetic and nonutilitarian uses of nature and wildlife. Although strong demographic segmentation implies continued oscillation in the political process, an overly aggressive interpretation of the current congressional mood could ultimately detach DoD from what appears to be a core American value and one that may continue to strongly affect the political process.

CONCLUSIONS

We answer the four policy questions above in the following manner:

1. DoD's current program is motivated by two goals: compliance
   with overarching laws and maintenance of the land for military

training. DoD now recognizes that there can be a complex interaction between these two objectives, which may include the need
for a broad interpretation of requirements. DoD has built an
inward-looking program that focuses on this complex problem. It
has not yet needed the outward-looking capabilities of the large
land management agencies that face intense public and constituent scrutiny.

2. Competition for federal lands in the West, regional habitat degradation in the East and on the Pacific Coast, and new scientific
   principles imply that core DoD military interests will be increasingly affected by natural resource concerns beyond the
   boundaries of DoD lands. When addressing these issues, DoD will
   be subject to far more intense political scrutiny than it experiences within the boundaries of its bases.

3. The 1994 election may signal a significant shift in the nation's approach to natural resource management. However, there is strong
   popular identification with natural resource values, and the new
   Congress does not seem to be moving quickly to drastically alter
   DoD's responsibilities. One outcome of this process may be to increase the span of DoD discretion, implying a greater need to develop analytical tools to support requests for flexibility.

4. The risks associated with downsizing the natural and cultural resource management program far outweigh the minimal savings
   that can be obtained. More generally, DoD can best manage uncertainty by expanding the analytical capabilities of the program.

There are three areas where DoD should expand its role and the tools
it uses for management. First, the tendency for bases to become
ecological islands implies the need for analysis of regional ecological
and political trends, additional awareness of the emerging science of
conservation biology, and the ability to translate the implications
into on-base natural resource management. Second, DoD's need to
utilize extended lands implies a need for cross-service regional analyses to ensure that all military airspace and land use options have
been exhausted. DoD will also need to develop a more sophisticated
approach to the process of formal environmental review and public
involvement than that required for land within existing boundaries.
And finally, the new Congress' interest in allowing greater regulatory

flexibility implies that DoD will need additional new ways to measure the impact of natural resource requirements on its mission.

In many ways, these are the types of capabilities that an idealized resource management agency would possess. Resource management agencies are (in theory) organized in a manner that allows for regional synthesis of agency activities, awareness of local and regional political processes, the use of national-level planning tools, and a more general outward orientation. Although DoD cannot be organized like a resource management agency, it can strive to develop analogous capabilities. We identify two broad sequential options:

1. *An Evolutionary Option:* Short of radical restructuring, DoD could provide bases with additional capabilities to expand both the substantive scope of the program and its institutional links. Individual bases need to be aware of resource availability on other bases in the region, and of developments in the habitats surrounding bases. At headquarters, a multidisciplinary policy planning team should be formed to conduct a broad range of analyses, support individual bases in identifying multiservice options, mediate military/natural resource issues in regions, and develop tools and models for better characterizing DoD's use of federal lands.

2. *A Radical Restructuring Option:* After implementing the evolutionary option, DoD should evaluate the potential for separating installation management (including natural resource management) from the military chain of command. There could be a regionally organized chain of command for installation support operations. This would facilitate development of regional perspectives and utilization of planning tools, while approximating the organizational design of a resource management agency. Even though this is consistent with our analysis of requirements for natural resource management, additional analysis of installation management issues and effects on the military mission would also be required.

Programatically, we recommend at the base level

- stabilizing and augmenting natural resource staffs at bases. These staffs have never reached sufficient numbers to properly address on-base management issues and are generally unprepared to cope with complex political environments.

- unifying natural resource funding to allow more flexibility for strategic planning and analysis and eliminate the need to conduct revenue-generating activities such as timber harvesting, grazing, agriculture, etc.

- developing a decisionmaking system and funding mechanism to allow bases to invest in off-base mitigation as appropriate.

- creating, on a pilot level, a new position at bases analogous to the base transition coordinator in base closure. This individual's job would be oriented toward those external issues that affect base natural resource management in the short or long run.

At a headquarters level, we recommend

- using the initial work from DoD's biodiversity dialogue to continue toward development of a "military conservation biology" that incorporates the principles of this new science while accounting for near-term programmatic requirements and limitations. This can be initiated by using one critical DoD installation to conduct a "model" natural resource planning exercise that incorporates the principles of ecosystem management and conservation biology in a DoD framework. This would consist of analysis of the base's role in the regional ecology and a description of the active management processes needed to achieve conservation goals at the base. A comprehensive land-use plan that incorporates all human (including mission) activities at the base would be required. Explicit analysis of how such an approach differs from the current "compliance-oriented" approach should be made.

- in developing a strategy for the future of the program, explicitly including consideration of the institutional and organizational investment that has occurred in the last 10 years to build the current adequate, but fragile, natural and cultural resource program.

- prioritizing resource management actions by identifying where on DoD's 25 million acres a close interaction among law, ecol-

ogy, and mission planning is required for successful land management and which lands serve as buffer zones or unusable terrain (from a military perspective) and thus require less-intense
management. However, the interactions between the two types
of land must be accounted for.

- expanding on the Air Force's new ranges and airspace planning
  office at headquarters by creating a multiservice policy planning
  office to conduct the tasks highlighted in the preceding discussion of the "evolutionary option." Its first task should be to review the processes for renewing the six major bases under the
  Military Lands Withdrawal Act and help ensure appropriately
  uniform approaches across the services.

- conducting a review of all DoD uses, and applications for use, of
  extended lands as a second task for the policy planning staff. The
  review should include National Guard uses—which are linked in
  the public's mind to active-force initiatives—and should be
  combined with a military needs assessment. This should lead to
  a systematic ranking of both military priorities and resource
  needs. Requests of relatively minor military importance that
  imply significant resource needs should be scrutinized.

- reviewing DoD policy toward Native American groups in recognition of the unique role Native Americans play among the
  groups competing for access to "extended lands" in the West.
  More-specific recommendations are provided in a companion
  report.[3]

- assigning a liaison to work with Bureau of Land Management
  personnel monitoring the status of withdrawn land and to
  increase DoD institutional knowledge of the land withdrawal
  process.

- conducting an Air Force–led "lessons-learned" analysis for the
  Idaho experience (since the Army's analysis of a natural resource
  management setback at Fort Bragg has proved to be invaluable).
  The objective of such an analysis should be to determine sys-

---

[3]D. Mitchell and D. Rubenson, *Native American Affairs and the Department of Defense,*
Santa Monica, Calif.: RAND, MR-630-OSD, 1996.

temic determinants of the problems rather than to focus on individual blame.

- exploring ways to promote organizational learning from the diverse NEPA processes conducted by DoD. This would at a minimum include a greater level of internal involvement in many environmental impact statement processes.

- expanding the current examination of life-cycle costs of new weapon systems, which has begun to consider costs of pollution and waste disposal, to incorporate land use and airspace needs.

Finally, we note that DoD's expanding involvement with natural and cultural resource management may represent a fundamental shift in the nature of its environmental responsibilities. While the decade between 1985 and 1995 was oriented toward the problems of hazardous wastes at DoD facilities, those problems have been largely solved in terms of the need for senior DoD policymakers to engage in and to develop new policy approaches. Expanding population and new military mission requirements imply that managing for resource scarcity is emerging as a new fundamental challenge. This challenge will require less financial investment than the problem of hazardous wastes, but it will require more time and attention of senior DoD management and will have a more direct impact on the military mission. *DoD's role in resource management and the nation's stake in that role involve "More Than 25 Million Acres."*

LIST OF ACRONYMS AND ABBREVIATIONS

BLM	Bureau of Land Management
BRAC	Base Realignment and Closure
CNRMP	Comprehensive Natural Resource Management Plan
CPSS	Columbia Plateau Shrub-Steppe
DoD	Department of Defense
DoE	Department of Energy
DoI	Department of the Interior
DPW	Directorate of Public Works
EIS	environmental impact statement
ESA	Endangered Species Act
FLPMA	Federal Land Policy and Management Act
FORPLAN	forest planning
F&W	U.S. Fish and Wildlife Service
GOLD	Greater Owyhee Legal Defense
INRMPs	Integrated Natural Resource Management Plans
ITAM	Integrated Training Area Management program
ITR	Idaho Training Range
MOU	Memorandum of Understanding
NEPA	National Environmental Policy Act
NFMA	National Forest Management Act
NPS	National Park Service
OEP	Office of Environmental Policy
RAMA	Rural Alliance for Military Accountability
RCW	red cockaded woodpecker

SANDAG	San Diego County Association of Governments
THAAD	Theater High-Altitude Area Defense System
USFS	U.S. Forest Service

Chapter One

THE BRIEFING

**More Than 25 Million Acres?
DoD as a Federal Natural and
Cultural Resource Manager**

RAND *MR715-1*

Figure 1

INTRODUCTION

The late 1990s will be a critical period for the Department of Defense's (DoD's) environmental program. The program has expanded rapidly in the last 10 years in response to community concerns about pollution from defense facilities. By the mid-1980s,

Congress had insisted, through both law and budget, that DoD respond to the problems of hazardous waste at defense installations. DoD built a large program as an "emergency response" to problems that had accumulated over decades.

The result was rapid growth in the DoD's environmental program at a time when the overall department was downsizing. From 1985 to 1995, the DoD's environmental program grew from less than $1 billion annually to more than $5 billion per year. Starting in the early 1990s, it became apparent that the program had to move beyond its emergency response origins and toward the role of solving DoD's long-term challenges with greater efficiency and purpose. The election of the 104th Congress, with its emphasis on budget reductions and a general review of environmental policy, brought greater urgency to these issues.

This report focuses on one aspect of DoD's $5-billion-per-year environmental program: the at most $200 million per-year program to manage natural and cultural resources on federal lands.[1] This program element was not the focus of the broad expansion in the mid-1980s, but it did develop and expand as a by-product of the greater regulatory scrutiny given to all DoD activities.

Several factors motivate this focus. Natural and cultural resource management is widely acknowledged to have a more direct impact on the military mission than other environmental program elements. While hazardous wastes affect communities and living conditions on a base, and may imply legal and financial obligations, they only occasionally have a direct impact on the military mission. In contrast, utilization of the land, skies, and water are integral to this mission. The significance of maintaining an effective, capable natural resource management program is often underemphasized in developing DoD policy.[2] The small program element for managing these re-

---

[1]There is significant uncertainty in providing a single budgetary figure for the DoD natural resource program, as many resource-related projects fall within DoD's legal compliance program and its environmental impact statements. $200 million represents our efforts to allocate those costs to natural and cultural resources, although formal DoD estimates are 25 to 50 percent lower.

[2]One example of a high-level strategic study that does include consideration of natural and cultural resource management is the "Report of the Defense Science Board Task Force on Environmental Security," April 22, 1995, Office of the Under Secretary of

sources could easily be decimated if it is included in a generalized downsizing. While DoD has not invested significant financial resources in the program, it has made a large investment in terms of organizational and command efforts to build the program and to cope with the close intersection between resource management and the military mission. Premature downsizing could mean this investment would have to be repeated at a later point, possibly at greater cost.

Perhaps the most significant motivation for this review is the contradictory and oscillatory forces guiding DoD's efforts to manage natural and cultural resources. The Clinton administration has embraced the conservation of biodiversity as a policy goal. Its policy instrument, ecosystem management, calls for federal agencies to consider problems in the context of *ecological* rather than federal agency boundaries. This has created significant anxiety within DoD because many believe the department should exclusively focus on problems within its boundaries. The election of the new Congress seems to represent an important reversal of these administration goals. It also suggests that the natural and cultural resource management program could be downsized.

RESEARCH QUESTIONS AND APPROACH

"More Than 25 Million Acres?"

DoD's obligation to conserve natural and cultural resources is motivated by forces both external and internal to the agency. Society places demands on DoD as expressed by law, policy, regulation, or even public outcry. DoD also has a need to share and participate in the broader goals and values held by the society it seeks to protect, and from which it draws its core strength. National-security-related exemptions from these externally created demands are granted only occasionally and with great caution. Conservation goals may also emerge from inside the department if resources are essential for conducting the military mission. At times, society's externally

---

Defense, Acquisition and Technology. However while citing natural resource–military mission interactions as the rationale for program review, the Defense Science Board report focused its recommendations almost entirely on waste compliance and cleanup issues.

mandated goals will affect conduct of the military mission, thus blurring the distinction between external and internal mandates.

As such, our general review of DoD's natural and cultural resource management program was motivated by two questions posed by a senior DoD policymaker:

1. What are the most important long-run scientific, demographic, legal, political, and ethical trends in American society that will affect DoD's natural and cultural resource program?

2. What near- and far-term programmatic steps should DoD undertake to respond to those trends?

At the time the research project was formulated, it appeared that the major external pressure was for DoD to expand its role in natural and cultural resource issues. In addition to ecosystem management, there was substantial policy interest in harnessing the capabilities of the DoD and applying those capabilities to a broad range of ecological issues.

During the course of our study, the 1994 congressional elections highlighted the importance of different values and forces. The new Congress expressed concern about diverting DoD funds to "nondefense" purposes and promised a general review of environmental policy from a utilitarian and development perspective.

Thus, rather than simply seeking to examine those forces encouraging a more expansive DoD role, we felt the need to reexamine the motivations that have produced DoD's current program, those that imply an expanded role and those that imply the potential to reduce DoD involvement in resource management. Overall, we seek to determine what is at stake in DoD's attempts to manage natural and cultural resources. Based on acreage alone, DoD's holdings (25 million acres) are small and represent only a small portion of federal lands. However, the title *More Than 25 Million Acres?* implies a symbolic question about the military, ecological, and political significance of this responsibility.

Approach

Obviously there is no concise or well-proven methodology for conducting such a review. Two earlier RAND studies[3] gave us experience with DoD's existing program and the current legal and political structures that govern many of its activities. We recast many of these findings to provide a summary of the forces that have produced DoD's current program. We also make a systematic comparison of this role with that of the large resource management agencies.

We used our past experience as a basis for targeting a series of emerging issues and trends for more careful analysis. We also supplemented this base of experience to distinguish how these trends will uniquely affect DoD, as opposed to how they will affect large land management agencies such as the U.S. Forest Service and the Bureau of Land Management.

An exploration of the findings of the emerging science of conservation biology provided an understanding of the views of this scientific community, which is quite prominent in the resource management debate. We also reviewed the Clinton administration's efforts to implement ecosystem management, which may represent the long-run political trend resulting from the principles of conservation biology. Two companion studies, one on trends in public opinion (which is unpublished and analyzed results of a series of U.S. public opinion surveys covering the last 25 years) and one on the emerging political significance of Native American interests in the resource management debate,[4] produced important contributions to complement the present report. We have also reviewed the debate taking place within the 104th Congress and attempted to identify its long-term implications.

To keep this review relevant to near-term decisions, we related these trends to DoD case studies, which were based on interviews and a

---

[3]David Rubenson, Jerry Aroesty, and Charles Thompsen, *Two Shades of Green: Environmental Protection and Combat Training,* Santa Monica, Calif.: RAND, R-4220-A, 1992, and David Rubenson, Jerry Aroesty, Pamela Wyn Wicinas, Gwen Farnsworth, and Kim Ramsey, *Marching to Different Drummers: Evolution of the Army's Environmental Program,* Santa Monica, Calif.: RAND, MR-453-A, 1994.

[4]D. Mitchell and D. Rubenson, *Native American Affairs and the Department of Defense,* Santa Monica, Calif.: RAND, MR-630-OSD, 1996.

review of legislative, executive, and administrative documents. The cases included the Yakima Training and Maneuver Area, the Mojave Desert Initiative, New Mexico DoD bases, Fort Carson (and the Piñon Canyon acquisition), Fort Bragg, Camp Pendleton, Idaho Training Range, and others. Since many questions considered in this report concern ecosystem and off-base resource management, two of our cases (those in Mojave and New Mexico) are broadly configured to assess regional issues and necessarily cut across several DoD installations. The cases were selected to include installations where environmental management issues both inside and outside of base boundaries were affecting base management, either because of regulatory, political, or legislated requirements. Western bases are emphasized to explore the effect of high regional population growth, and in recognition of the importance of the western region for future DoD expansion and renewals of withdrawn land.

The cases differed in terms of the regulatory requirements and the political environment faced by each installation. This is one of the fundamental challenges for DoD natural and cultural resource management: to provide flexible management to deal with various environments. While the diversity in cases introduces a large number of independent variables that cannot be controlled for, this was determined to be an appropriate study design to develop policy recommendations that could address the actual diversity of the management challenge. Given this variation across cases, interviews were open-ended and not structured to be identical for each case. Interviews were conducted with DoD personnel at various levels, with representatives of nongovernmental organizations, and with legislative staff.

As we progressed to the stage of linking external societal trends to DoD programmatic concerns, our question relating to expanded roles for the DoD became nearly identical to the issue of whether DoD needs to engage in managing natural and cultural resources beyond the boundaries of its bases—or more than the 25 million acres presently managed by the DoD.

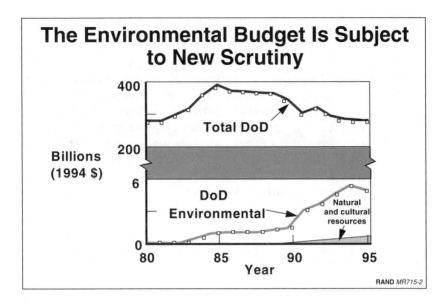

Figure 2

Figure 2 highlights the fiscal motivation for a broad-based review of DoD's natural and cultural resource management program. The DoD environmental program has not followed overall DoD funding trends and has been one of the few DoD programs to grow during the last 10 years. Only in FY 1995 and 1996 did overall environmental funding begin to decline.

The largest element of the DoD environmental program has been cleanup and control of hazardous waste. Congress has strongly voiced its intention to reduce the annual expenditures for these activities, and although there are still vast cleanup obligations to be fulfilled, some of which are legally mandated, the expected reduction points to a fundamental change in DoD's environmental challenge. By implementing cleanup remedies at some sites, by addressing community concerns at others, and by recognizing that remedies may not exist at still others, many of the conceptual aspects of cleanup and control have largely been resolved in terms of the need for attention by senior DoD policymakers. A system has been put in place that allows the department to fulfill its obligations.[5]

There has been far less analytical thinking and policy attention given to DoD's natural resource obligations, which at most total only $200 million of the entire environmental budget. However, there is a direct connection with mission effectiveness. Also, the small size of this program element implies it could be significantly affected by a generalized downsizing of the environmental program. Thus, *More Than 25 Million Acres?* is a question that asks whether it is becoming necessary for DoD policymakers to give increased attention to the department's natural and cultural resource management obligations.

_____

[5]One exception to this conclusion is the problem of cleanup, transfer, and reuse of closing military bases. In our judgment, this problem still requires the attention of senior DoD policymakers and even Congress.

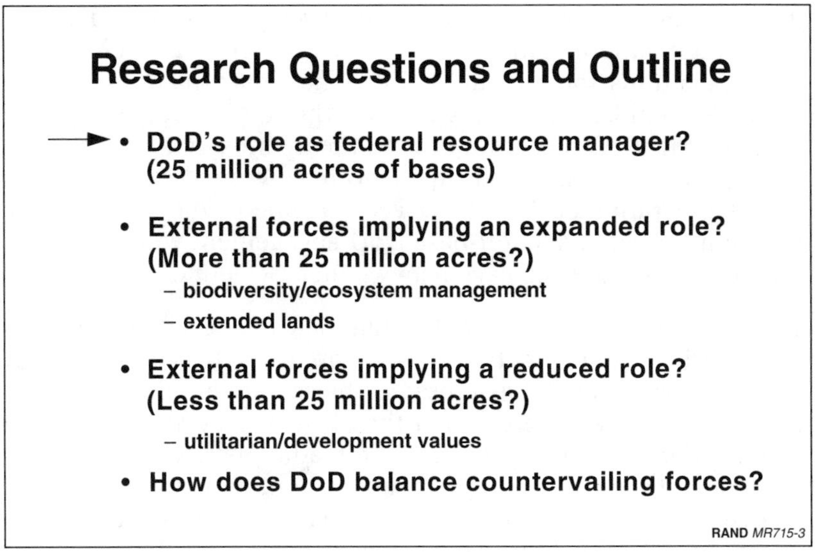

Research Questions and Outline

⟶ • **DoD's role as federal resource manager?**
   (25 million acres of bases)

• **External forces implying an expanded role?**
  (More than 25 million acres?)
  – biodiversity/ecosystem management
  – extended lands

• **External forces implying a reduced role?**
  (Less than 25 million acres?)

  – utilitarian/development values

• **How does DoD balance countervailing forces?**

RAND *MR715-3*

Figure 3

Figure 3 displays the research questions that are both the focus and outline of this report.

The budget trends highlighted in Figure 2 provide sufficient motivation for a review of DoD's natural and cultural resource management program. Even without new external forces, DoD will be forced to make decisions regarding future program direction and funding. Our first goal is therefore to review the mechanisms of governance, rationales, and capabilities of the existing program, which involves management of the 25 million acres of DoD bases. We discuss the mechanisms society has put in place to govern DoD's efforts to conduct the military mission while conserving natural and cultural resources.

We then analyze external factors pointing toward a more demanding resource management role and place them in the context of the current program. As mentioned in the discussion following Figure 1, through an iterative process we found the question of an expanded role to be similar to the question of a DoD role beyond existing base boundaries; hence the question, *More Than 25 Million Acres?* Our investigation is divided into two subsections: one centered around the Clinton administration's policy of ecosystem management and its implications for regional habitat management, the other on "extended lands." By this we mean the lands affected by DoD airspace use, DoD use of waterways, those lands that DoD may use on a special basis, and lands that DoD may seek to acquire. We examine the rationale for off-base engagement and compare the mechanisms that affect off-base DoD engagement with those governing DoD resource management within base boundaries.

We then turn our attention to the utilitarian and development values and priorities highlighted by the election of the 104th Congress. At this point, it is impossible to predict the extent, duration, and durability of the new congressional thrust, which by some measures stands in direct contrast to the Clinton administration's approach. Some feel it may allow downsizing of the natural and cultural resource management program in a similar manner as was done for hazardous waste programs; hence the question, *Less than 25 million acres?* We highlight both the reasons for this interpretation as well as the risks of misreading the recent political signals.

Finally, we seek to develop a strategy that appropriately balances budget constraints and the two countervailing trends of placing importance on ecological issues and downsizing programs that address them.

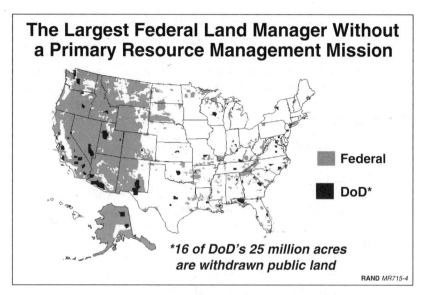

The Largest Federal Land Manager Without a Primary Resource Management Mission

Federal

DoD*

*16 of DoD's 25 million acres
are withdrawn public land

RAND MR715-4

Figure 4

Figure 4 presents a map of the approximately 650 million acres of all federal lands and the 25 million acres managed by DoD. The Army manages approximately 12 million acres, the Air Force 9 million, and the Navy 3 million. Not included in the total are the lands of the Civil Works Division of the Army Corps of Engineers.[6] Most federal land is located in the western United States, with the two largest land management agencies, the United States Forest Service (USFS) and the Bureau of Land Management (BLM) managing the bulk of the holdings in large parcels. DoD's lands are scattered across the country and represent the largest chunk of federal lands in some regions.

As illustrated by the title of Figure 4, DoD is a unique federal land manager.[7] In contrast to the BLM, the USFS, the National Park

---

[6]The Army Corps of Engineers civil works projects include an additional 10 million acres of land.

[7]It is interesting to note that in the Wilderness Society's book by D. Zaslowsky and T. Watkins, *These American Lands* (Island Press, 1994), the history, culture, and legal

Service (NPS), and the U.S. Fish and Wildlife Service (F&W), DoD does not have a primary resource management mission. Traditionally, BLM's mission has been supporting constituent use of the land for activities such as hunting, fishing, grazing, mining, timber harvesting, off-road vehicle use, and other utilitarian needs. The Forest Service was oriented toward timber harvesting and management for sustained yield of timber products.

During the last two decades, the emphasis on commodity production and utilitarian use has come under increased scrutiny and has given way to the management doctrine known as "multiple use." Multiple use is a philosophy that assigns value to nonutilitarian uses of the land, including biodiversity, cultural resources, or simply preserving scenic vistas. The doctrine, which has been codified in law, calls upon the BLM and the USFS to respect multiple-use values and manage accordingly. It is plausible that the Clinton administration's vision of "ecosystem management" could ultimately evolve into a fundamental philosophy that succeeds "multiple use."

In addition to the BLM and USFS, the Fish and Wildlife Service manages 91 million acres of federal wildlife sanctuaries. The primary mission for these lands has been conservation (originally motivated by the desire to support hunting activities), though they have historically (and controversially) been used for a wide range of utilitarian purposes. Also, the National Park Service manages approximately 76 million acres of land and oddly comes closer to mirroring DoD's task than other agencies. Its holdings are widely scattered, and its mission contains a dual objective of preserving wildlife and aesthetic values while providing service to visitors and the public at large. However, unlike for the DoD task, it is ultimately the condition of the land that makes the parks attractive for visitors and is the yardstick by the which the National Park Service is measured.

DoD does not have a primary resource management mission, and its military mission has a varied and shifting dependence on land use. At times, training is enhanced by conserving biota on training grounds. Factors such as weapons technology, military doctrine, simulation capability, or type of threat can act to increase or de-

---

basis for each federal land management agency—except DoD—is discussed. DoD is never mentioned.

crease dependence on, and intensity of, land use. Although society does insist on some "multiple-use" management (as will be discussed later), DoD's military performance is not measured by its role as a land manager.

One overlooked fact is that most DoD lands (16 of the 25 million acres) are "withdrawn" public land. This land was previously in the public domain and has been withdrawn for DoD use, generally by act of Congress. The conditions for withdrawals vary. While White Sands Missile Range in New Mexico and other withdrawals may be withdrawn in perpetuity, the withdrawal terms can be amended to 20 years by a mandated review motivated by the Federal Land Policy and Management Act (FLPMA), rather than by statutory changes. If this review is ever completed, all of BLM's recommendations from the review will be considered by Congress, providing Congress more opportunity to apply specific resource management requirements to DoD.[8] DoD is obliged to assume land management responsibility for withdrawn lands, with the exception of a few cases for which land management authority (or specific aspects of land management) is explicitly ascribed to the Department of the Interior (DoI). Since all withdrawn lands could eventually revert back to the DoI, some effort is made by the Secretary of the Interior to monitor the uses and status of withdrawn military lands. Given BLM's limited budgets and tradition of little involvement in managing military lands, such monitoring efforts are modest.

---

[8]The statutory deadline has passed for completion of this review under Section 204(1) of FLPMA. The authors are grateful to Dwight Hempel, Military Programs Coordinator of the Bureau of Land Management, for bringing this to our attention.

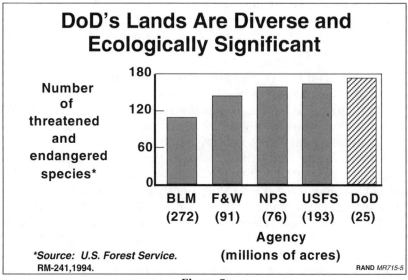

Figure 5

Figure 5 highlights little-known and remarkable data that illustrate the importance and difficulty of DoD's resource management challenge. DoD lands are among the most biologically diverse and ecologically significant lands in the nation. Despite managing only 25 million acres, DoD has roughly more federally listed threatened and endangered species on its lands than on those of any other agency.[9]

The reasons behind the totals in Figure 5 are numerous. DoD lands are surveyed more intensely than other lands, and the geographical distribution of DoD lands exceeds that of other agencies.[10] The large number of endangered species is also a result of the limited outside access to DoD lands, the benign impact of some military training (relative to commodity production occurring on other federal land),

---

[9]The Nature Conservancy's Heritage Data Base places DoD's total as the third largest behind that of the NPS and the USFS. See *Conserving Biodiversity on Military Lands— A Technical Framework*, p. 1-13, February 1995, The U.S. Department of Defense, The Nature Conservancy, and The Keystone Center.

[10]See pages 1-15 and 1-16 of *Conserving Biodiversity* for documentation of the diversity of DoD lands.

and DoD's management of the only federal tracts in some parts of the country. DoD lands are essentially the only federal lands for certain ecosystems, such as the long-leaf pine ecosystem in the Southeast, the coastal sage in southern California, Hawaiian ecosystems, and others.[11]

The ecological significance of DoD lands poses a complex problem in balancing priorities. DoD trains on lands that society also values for conservation and other environmental reasons, and in the last 10 years, society has asked DoD to bring greater emphasis to the conservation side of the equation. Conversely, Congress may now be signaling DoD to place greater emphasis on military concerns. These opposing signals clearly complicate the process of formulating DoD's long-term programmatic response.

In the following charts, we explore how society has expressed its desire for DoD to conserve natural and cultural resources while conducting its military mission. We then discuss the implementation of this guidance and identify emerging issues and challenges.

---

[11]Hawaii itself contains 224 listed endangered species, about 15 percent of the national total, *The New York Times*, May 16, 1995, p. B7.

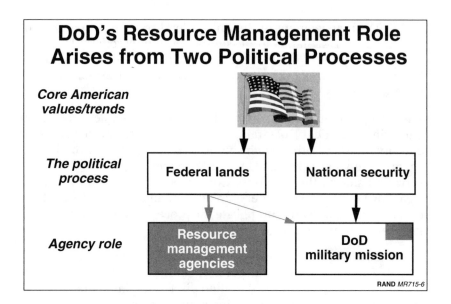

Figure 6

Figure 6 provides a simple model of the process that governs DoD's military mission and its management of natural and cultural resources. We assume that a set of core values and trends defines the political process in the United States. Such core values are partially spelled out in the Constitution but are far broader and are difficult to define or measure precisely. We also assume those core values are influenced and altered by changes in science, technology, demography, and other fundamental social forces. It is ultimately the responsibility of the political process to translate those values into practical laws and policies.

Our definition of the political process includes all influences outside an agency that govern that agency's activity. At a minimum, this means laws, policies, executive orders, guidance, and budgets formulated in Congress or the White House. It might also mean applicable state laws and policies. Internal department policy or regulations are assumed to arise at the level of "agency role."

A defining characteristic of DoD's role is the (largely) distinct political processes governing military and conservation activities. DoD's military mission is governed by the President with a significant degree of congressional oversight, especially in the budget process. There has historically been a broad, national consensus about military security needs, and those outside DoD who are responsible for its governance generally have experience with and knowledge of DoD. Since the DoD is the largest agency chartered to carry out a national security mission, the political process of defining military policy necessarily includes DoD personnel as important, active, vocal, and influential participants.

DoD is also subject to the outcomes of a political process centered around the BLM and the USFS—a process in which DoD is at best a minor participant. Far more diverse interests participate in this process as compared with the national security political process. Not only do Congress and the President debate laws and policies, but the private constituents of the land management agencies, the states, and the public are also involved. States can pass laws that are enforceable on federal lands, and many of the laws governing federal land use explicitly include roles for public and constituent participation. Federal lands are also affected by a broad array of environmental laws and policies that have been designed for federal agencies and all other public and private institutions.

In Figure 6, the darkened box in the DoD military mission box represents DoD's natural and cultural resource program and indicates its primary role of military mission support. Although the connection between federal lands and the military mission (the diagonal line in Figure 6) has formally existed for more than 25 years, in practical terms it is only 10 years old. There was little to no enforcement of these priorities on DoD lands prior to the mid-1980s. In its absence, the natural resources support function was "in practice" limited to maintaining those natural resource features required for military training, such as ensuring that training lands did not suffer significant erosion or loss of vegetative cover. However, even this role was minimized by a sense of unlimited land and the urgency of military training. Those responsible for the military mission had little interest in long-term maintenance of training land, and the natural resources support office had few internal or external constituents. This office's activities were oriented toward timber harvesting and grazing on DoD lands and the return of the associated revenues to support continued existence of the natural resources program.

Since the mid-1980s, new legal obligations for natural and cultural resource management have emerged, and these need to be satisfied in a manner that minimizes negative effects on the military mission. These new obligations involve some changes in cultural resource protection laws, such as new amendments to the National Historic Preservation Act, but mainly involve a greater level of enforcement of already existing laws. However, as will be discussed in the next figure, the DoD still receives significantly less guidance from the "federal lands" process than do the resource management agencies. The connection between the two remains an afterthought in the political process for federal lands.

This lack of detail in political guidance has led to sharp discussion within DoD about the extent to which DoD's natural resource management program should look toward societal values and trends (notionally the flag in Figure 6) for guidance. This is occasionally referred to as "doing the right thing" in some discussions involving DoD natural resource personnel. It involves the question of whether or not legal compliance sufficiently defines DoD resource management goals. This complex question will be discussed in the following figures.

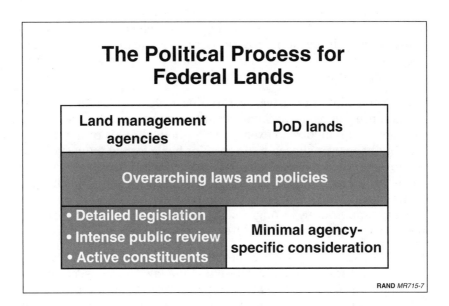

Figure 7

Figure 7 examines the box in Figure 6 representing the political process for federal lands and highlights a broad distinction between
DoD and traditional land management agencies.

OVERARCHING LAWS AND POLICIES

The diagonal line in Figure 6 refers essentially to the overarching
laws and policies relevant to all federal agencies. Most notable (in
terms of specific obligations) among the overarching laws and policies relevant to all federal agencies are the National Environmental
Policy Act (NEPA), which requires environmental review of all new
federal or federally funded activities, and the Endangered Species Act
(ESA), which protects individual species (and their habitats) listed by
the Fish and Wildlife Service as threatened or endangered. Some
federal laws require consultation and planning with federal and/or

state officials.[12]   Other "overarching laws" relevant to natural resources include certain provisions of the Clean Water Act, the
Migratory Bird Treaty Act, the National Historic Preservation Act,
some state statutes, and many other laws.

Two of the most pervasive overarching laws, NEPA and the ESA,
contain provisions for national security exemptions. The Secretary
of Defense can invoke an exemption to the ESA at his or her discretion but has never chosen to do so. Nor has a formal request of this
nature from the services reached the Secretary's desk. The President
can grant an exemption from NEPA and did so for some specific activities during the Persian Gulf War and for actions taken in the wake
of Hurricane Andrew. Congress has also exempted certain parts of
the Base Realignment and Closure (BRAC) process from NEPA.

In addition to natural resource law, there is a wide variety of laws relevant to cultural resources. These include laws for conserving historic buildings, conserving archaeological resources, and protecting
Native American artifacts, sacred sites, and rights of way. As with
many laws affecting natural resources, enforcement of these laws often requires a citizen law suit since there is no formal regulatory
agency charged with enforcement. The laws generally mandate self-
enforcement by each agency.

One of the most significant new overarching policies has been the
Clinton administration's initiatives in ecosystem management.
These policies challenge all federal agencies to look beyond their
particular political boundaries and consider the interactive ecological effects within and across ecosystems. As with most overarching
policies, the primary consideration has been the large land management agencies. However, DoD is included in "all federal agencies,"
and the White House has explicitly recognized DoD's potential role.

---

[12]The National Historic Preservation Act and the Endangered Species Act contain
provisions for consultation with state government representatives.

AGENCY-SPECIFIC LAWS AND POLICIES

BLM and USFS

Although DoD is subject to the same overarching laws and policies as
the resource management agencies, it receives far less external oversight for land management. The resource agencies are governed by
agency-specific "organic acts," which provide detailed rules and
formal planning procedures that specify methods for incorporating
public input. The National Forest Management Act (NFMA) is the
organic act for the U.S. Forest Service, and the Federal Land Policy
and Management Act of 1976 (FLPMA) governs the activities of the
Bureau of Land Management. NFMA mandates that the USFS engage in a nearly continuous cycle of formal forest planning known as
FORPLAN.[13] FORPLAN is aimed at synthesizing and summing all
forest activities at the local level into a national vision of forest use.
FLPMA has a similar but less-elaborate planning mandate but also
contains detailed prescriptions concerning BLM land utilization.

Although BLM and the USFS are the largest landholders, NPS and
F&W also maintain large holdings, with the former engaged in constant tension between ecological conservation and making the parks
accessible to visitors. This tension is embedded in the Organic Act of
1916, which guides the park's overall mission. A wide range of laws
governs the activities of the F&W in its role as manager of the
nation's wildlife refuges.[14]

In addition to agency-specific laws, public and constituent scrutiny
of the land management agencies is far more intense than for DoD
lands. Public users are numerous, varied, organized, and capable of
utilizing the political process to influence agency decisions. Since
BLM and USFS lands are public resources, communities actively organize to influence BLM and USFS decisionmaking.

---

[13]For a summary of the USFS planning process, see Office of Technology Assessment,
*Forest Service Planning: Accommodating Uses, Producing Outputs, and Sustaining
Ecosystems,* OTA-F-505, February 1992.

[14]See Zaslowsky and Watkins for a good summary of the F&W role as well as that for
all land management agencies except DoD.

DoD

In contrast, DoD bases are subject to little outside scrutiny beyond enforcement mechanisms for the overarching laws.[15]   DoD's arguably most significant controversy, which involved the red cockaded woodpecker at Fort Bragg, was largely a dispute between regulators and the Army with only minimal public involvement. Although there has been significant public interest in DoD's program for hazardous waste management, there has not been a similar outcry regarding the natural and cultural resource management of military lands. The public still has an "off limits" view of military lands even though access is unrestricted in many cases.

The most significant "agency-specific" policy affecting DoD land management to date (beyond the previously mentioned national security exemptions) is the Legacy program, which was established in 1990. Congress initially set aside $10 million per year for five years for DoD to undertake activities to identify, conserve, and protect natural and cultural resources on DoD lands. Legacy is not tied to legal compliance, and one view is that it should be used for conservation activities reflecting care American values but not implied by law on military mission. Congress has consistently added additional funds to the Legacy budget, and in the past three years, this program has been budgeted at $50 million per year. However, at this time Legacy is under great scrutiny, and current indications are that it will be budgeted at $10 million for FY 1996.

A potentially important agency-specific law is the Sikes Act. Passed by Congress in 1960, the act called for approval of hunting and fishing programs by state and federal officials in order for installations to establish these programs and collect fees for use. The Sikes Act was amended in 1986 to ensure that (1) trained professional staff manage the fish and wildlife program, (2) fish and wildlife plans are reviewed, and (3) timber sales are compatible with fish and wildlife plans. Congress is currently considering amendments that would (1) mandate that fish and wildlife plans be replaced by broader Integrated Natural Resource Management Plans (INRMPs), (2) mandate formal

---

[15]We should note that the ecological value of DoD land was highlighted in *The New York Times* on January 2, 1996, p. B5, one of the few such articles in a widely publicized forum.

reviews of the INRMPs, possibly by states and the Fish and Wildlife Service, (3) mandate adequate staffing to fulfill the act, and (4) authorize appropriations. If a bill survives in this form, it will bring a new level of congressional specificity to DoD land management, though still far less detailed than NFMA or FLPMA. However, at the time this report is being written, the future of the amended Sikes Act is unknown.

Finally, some of the laws authorizing the withdrawals of public lands for military purposes require specific management approaches, although enforcement to date has been minimal.

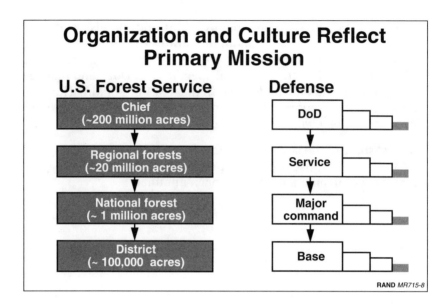

Figure 8

As illustrated in Figure 8, DoD and the land management agencies are organized around core missions and key constituents. The USFS is organized geographically, with each layer of management responsible for a greater quantity of forest acreage. This structure has obvious advantages for conducting resource management. Agency activities can be synthesized at different levels and planning tools can be developed and utilized at the national level to facilitate policy discussions and descriptions of agency problems and perspectives.

Implicit in the picture of the USFS organization is a perspective of looking outward toward the public and constituents. The regional structure provides a close connection between the jobs of managers at different levels and the communities they live in. The large size of USFS holdings implies that the service may often be an important participant in regional ecological planning. In addition, a typical FORPLAN contains detailed protocols for incorporating public input and synthesizing data at different levels of aggregation.

In contrast, DoD is organized for its military mission and is geographically fragmented across the four military services, the major commands, and the subcommands. Two bases in close geographic proximity may be separated widely in the chain of command. The DoD structure does not facilitate coordination on natural resources up and down the chain of command, or across it to different bases in similar regions or ecosystems.[16]

Even though precise organizational designs vary among services, commands, and even among individual bases, we use the largest box under defense (containing DoD) in Figure 8 to represent the military function. The highest-ranking officer at an installation is typically responsible for both the military mission and installation (including resource) management. However, the reward structure is clearly oriented toward the military mission, with support functions delegated to a lower-ranking military officer who commands numerous directorates (represented by each of the small boxes following the DoD box in the figure). The Directorate of Public Works (DPW) contains the environmental program among other functions. The natural and cultural resource program (represented by the smallest, shaded box following the DoD box) resides within the environmental program and is therefore many layers beneath the installation commander. Typically, installation support functions are carried out by a permanent civilian staff commanded by a small number of military officers.

Each level reports upward to the highest-ranking officer at the installation and ultimately to the installation commander. That commander reports to a military commander at the major command level who is supported by a similar set of functional offices in a similar organizational relationship. There is no chain of command for support functions including installation management, environmental programs, or resource management.

Thus, DoD's natural resource program is fragmented. The result is a highly dispersed effort with minimal institutional capability to integrate and synthesize agency activities in geographic regions, or to monitor and evaluate the ways in which DoD uses its 25 million

---

[16]DoD has recently moved to establish a few regional environmental offices, although the relationship to the chain of command is not yet clear and will need several years to evolve. In all likelihood, these offices will dedicate most of their resources to hazardous waste cleanup and compliance issues.

acres. The organizational design also fosters a strong degree of isolation in the natural resources program.[17]

---

[17]The difficulties implied for environmental management are discussed in detail in MR-453-A, RAND, 1994.

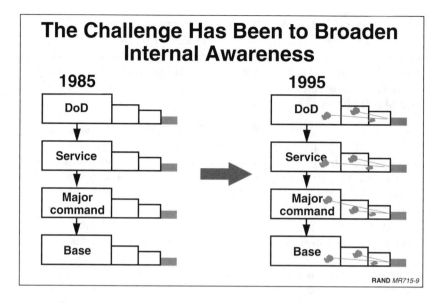

Figure 9

Figure 9 illustrates the changes within DoD that have occurred since the mid-1980s. Prior to the mid-1980s, resource management was a largely independent program attached to the DoD organization. The lack of outside regulatory scrutiny and the perception by military trainers that the land was inexhaustible left the natural resource function isolated from both internal and external forces. Over the past 10 years, the DoD has developed internal relationships and capabilities for resource management in response to enforcement of the overarching laws, particularly the Endangered Species Act. This is graphically illustrated in Figure 9 by the "patches," which represent natural and cultural resource interest, and by the connecting "informal organizational" lines.

FORT BRAGG

The opening of DoD lands and installations in the mid-1980s to regulatory inspection was largely motivated by the hazardous waste problem. Enforcement of the overarching natural and cultural resource laws (the Endangered Species Act, the National

Environmental Policy Act, the National Historic Preservation Act, Section 404 Clean Water Act, etc.) was slower in developing. These laws are generally a matter of an agency's self-enforcement and citizen law suit, rather than regulatory inspection. However, one dramatic act of enforcement occurred at Fort Bragg with the imposition of ESA-related military training restrictions.[18]

The experience at Fort Bragg from 1988 to 1992 demonstrated that DoD's natural resource program did not have the experience and political skills to cope with a conflict between natural resource law and the military mission. At Fort Bragg, the natural resource office was isolated from other base functions, and the Army was unprepared for the ESA process, which calls for negotiations and development of an endangered species plan with the U.S. Fish and Wildlife Service. The isolated natural resource office had neither the authority nor the skills to coordinate conservation efforts with military trainers. The natural resource office's traditional focus on timber harvesting further complicated the task of balancing species protection with the military mission. As a result, the restrictions imposed by the U.S. Fish and Wildlife Service were not optimized to simultaneously achieve species protection and minimize effects on military training.

THE MILITARY-ECOLOGY-LEGAL INTERACTION

Fort Bragg and other cases with similar but less dramatic results led the department to recognize a close interaction among natural resource laws, military training, and conservation of natural and cultural resources. To cope with possible conflicts, new internal linkages and capabilities were needed. The natural resource function had to change its orientation from revenue generation to compliance with natural resource law. Other components, including the base public works function (under which a natural resource office typically works), the garrison commander, and the military trainers themselves, had to understand the impact of their activities on natu-

---

[18]For a complete discussion of the process that occurred at Fort Bragg and its implications for the Army and its natural resource program, see R-4220-A, RAND, 1992. Also discussed is the deceptively strict regulatory structure of natural and cultural resource law.

ral and cultural resources and the need for their participation in conservation planning. Perhaps more significant, there was a requirement for each component to better comprehend the others' needs and values.

We should point out that not all DoD natural resource management obligations involve a complex internal interaction among law, ecology, and the military mission. Vast tracts of DoD land provide buffer zones for testing and overflight and involve only a minimal overlay of natural resource concerns and mission. Strong interaction is most prevalent for the Army and Marine Corps, both of which conduct intensive ground military missions. However, even in Forces Command (the Army's major command, which maintains the trained and ready units) only about 2 million of its 5 million acres of land are used for ground combat training.[19] The remainder is used for mission support or does not contain terrain suitable for combat training.

The different ways in which the military-ecology-legal interaction manifests itself further differentiates the DoD from the other land management agencies. Other land management agencies invest their efforts across large tracts of lands with valuable resources, but DoD must focus its natural resource management program on those tracts of land where the military-ecology-legal interaction is most intense. The approximately 300,000 acres at Camp Pendleton and Fort Bragg, where two of DoD's most important missions are conducted in sensitive ecosystems, may require as much organizational attention as several million of acres of other ecologically rich DoD lands. Headquarters has not yet developed the tools to fully distinguish priorities using this type of categorization.

------

[19]Remarks made by Dr. R. Shaw during his presentation at the "21st Environmental Symposium & Exhibition," American Defense Preparedness Association, April 18–20, 1995, San Diego, California.

A FRAGILE PROGRAM?

The Transfer of Integrated Training Army Management, Program Rationales, and Core Values

The lines within the boxes in Figure 9 are intended to illustrate the significant strides DoD has made in identifying important internal linkages and in building the internal capabilities to manage them. There is now increased awareness throughout DoD about the mission criticality of natural resources. One indication of this heightened sensitivity is the recent Army decision to shift proponency for the Integrated Training Army Management (ITAM) program, a broad-based management program element that emphasizes monitoring and restoration of vegetative cover and soil quality by the operators themselves.[20] This will make the users of the land directly responsible for its maintenance and the costs of restoration and recovery. It also represents a recognition by the operators that long-term training-land maintenance is essential for the military mission. However, this transfer also represents a significant test in the internal evolution of the organization. Military commanders will now be free to make an explicit budgetary trade-off between near-term readiness and the long-term need to maintain training lands. The transfer of responsibility is based on the conclusion that there has been sufficient cultural change to allow this trade-off to be managed by military commanders. However, this shift is occurring at a time of financial stress, and it will be important to monitor its implementation.

This transfer of responsibility brings into focus one of the most complex aspects of DoD's management program: the inherent difficulty in compartmentalizing the rationales for DoD natural and cultural resource management. The Army's management program is now divided largely into two well-defined subcategories, ITAM (which is support for military training) and compliance with the overarching natural resource laws. When ITAM was managed by the natural resource staff, it was often used to fulfill a wide range of other

---

[20]Examples of the linkage between vegetative cover and erosion concerns with the military mission can be found in *ITAM Bulletin,* US Army Construction Engineering Research Laboratory. See for example Vol. 95(1), which discusses concealment at Fort Riley and erosion at Fort Jackson.

conservation objectives that could not be scrupulously rationalized as fulfilling compliance or training objectives. However, this "fuzziness" is consistent with the general nature of natural and cultural resource law and the very long timelines under which natural resource problems develop and ultimately affect core military concerns. It is also consistent with the recognition that the condition of military lands can affect the public perception of DoD. The recent transfer of ITAM may represent a logical step in organizational evolution, but it will be a challenge to ensure that the concept of maintaining the land for military training is interpreted in properly broad terms.[21]

DoD is not alone in facing the problem of determining if there is a need to broadly interpret natural resource law and guidance.[22] It is almost impossible for Congress to prescribe all agency activities, and there is often significant latitude in how agencies interpret core American values. However, the nature of natural resource law and the lack of guidance given to DoD exacerbate the problem. The problem is also made more difficult by the many natural and cultural resource activities that may actually have no connection to compliance or training. Here DoD needs to determine the extent to which engagement in such activities is consistent with core American values. DoD must also weigh conflicting signals from the administration, which has encouraged natural and cultural resource conservation, and Congress—which, by reducing funding for Legacy, is asking DoD to dedicate fewer resources to such program activities.

Funding and Personnel

Today the DoD natural resource program is functional though fragile. The ITAM transfer is one example of that fragility. A stable funding mechanism for the program has never been developed, and five uncertain sources form a financial patchwork: (1) Legacy, the

---

[21]We must credit the Army for at least initially recognizing this need. The new *Integrated Area Management (ITAM) Program Strategy,* Headquarters, Department of the Army, 17 August 1995, places the needs of combat trainers within a broad framework of natural resource issues.

[22]See Evan J. Ringquist, "Political Control and Policy Impact in EPA's Office of Water Quality," *American Journal of Political Science,* 39(2):336–363, 1995, for a discussion of the need of agencies to look toward core American values and principles.

congressionally mandated fund for conservation of natural and cultural resources on DoD lands, which is the subject of intense congressional scrutiny and is now at the end of its initial five-year authorization, (2) compliance funds that were created to meet violations of hazardous waste laws and their highly prescriptive standards but that can, with some difficulty, be used for meeting the requirements of natural resource law, (3) funds from revenue-generating activities on DoD lands, such as grazing, timber, hunting, and agriculture (these activities are holdovers from the pre-1985 period and may produce adverse environmental effects. They have at times been terminated because of the conflict with the dual land management goals of legal compliance and military training), (4) base operations funds, which depend on the priorities of the individual commander and compete with funds for other base support activities, and (5) ITAMs for the Army.

In addition to funding uncertainty, the current program is also vulnerable from a human resources perspective. Having grown in importance during the last 10 years, the entire environmental function expanded at a time when the prevailing overall trend was to make more extensive use of contractors and build less dependence on permanent federal employees. As such, natural resource staffs have never reached numbers consistent with their new responsibilities and still do not have sufficient authority to interact with numerous other functions at the base.[23]

---

[23]For a discussion of staffing concerns see R-4220-A, RAND, 1992, pp. 16–18, and MR-453-A, RAND, 1994, pp. 63–64. An internal Navy memorandum in late 1992 indicated that there were only 83 positions Navy-wide for natural resource professionals. The memo also indicated that efforts to improve environmental staffs had not affected natural resource staffs. Staffing was also highlighted as a top problem area in a 1992 internal survey of the Air Force natural and cultural resources program. Overall, downsizing trends have only exacerbated these problems.

Program Status

- **Functional, fragile, inward looking**
- **Two convincing rationales:**
  - comply with law
  - support military mission
- **Conservation activities can:**
  - directly support compliance and mission
  - indirectly support them
  - enhance ecological values
- **Broad DoD support to go beyond "directly support"**
- **Responsive to new external forces?**

RAND *MR715-10*

Figure 10

Figure 10 summarizes our review of DoD's current natural and cultural resource management program. Despite fragility in terms of funding, personnel, and organizational commitment, DoD can take significant pride in its progress over the last 10 years and in its increased awareness of environmental impacts at all levels of the organization. This achievement was built on several painful setbacks and has required significant attention from both senior military leadership and civilian political leadership.

The current program's strong inward focus is justified by both the complexity of managing the military-legal-ecology intersection and the lack of outside public scrutiny as compared with large land management agencies.

Within DoD, two rationales prove convincing for natural and cultural resource management. The first involves compliance with the law or overarching policy. The second involves activities that support military training, such as erosion control, maintenance of vegetative cover, and maintenance of roads and trails. Given the complex interaction with compliance issues, this management has also come to represent a broad array of conservation activities.

DoD's natural and cultural resource problems can be roughly divided into three categories. Activities that have a clear and direct relationship to military training or compliance enjoy widespread institutional support. Other issues may seem unrelated but may ultimately affect both goals. These activities currently enjoy significant support within DoD, but it is uncertain how durable and deep this support may be. Obviously, there are other conservation activities that may enhance the ecology but may seem separable from compliance and training. DoD may want to engage in some of these activities to ensure public support, connectivity with basic societal values, and because of the difficulty in identifying which activities truly fall in this category.

Finally, we note that the transition depicted in Figure 9 developed in response to external regulatory pressures that were not anticipated by the DoD during the past 10 years. The department's response was made more problematic in that there were few explicit attempts to identify the character, strength, and direction of the forces driving the transition.

An explicit analysis of the factors that may influence further changes in DoD's natural and cultural resource program may help avoid or minimize such difficulties in the future. Of particular concern are emerging influences *external* to the department that may stress the effective, but inward-looking, organizational design. These emerging issues are described and assessed below.

Outline

- **DoD's role (25 million acres of bases)**

➤ • **An expanded role? (*More than 25 million acres?*)**
  - biodiversity/ecosystem management
  - extended lands

- **A reduced role? (*Less than 25 million acres?*)**
  - utilitarian/development values
- **How does DoD balance countervailing forces?**

RAND *MR715-11*

Figure 11

Figure 11 shows a condensed version of the outline presented in Figure 3. In the following pages, we examine emerging external forces that may point to an expanded DoD role. We seek to determine if the demand comes from military concern or from ecological concerns. In the latter case, we attempt to determine the nature of the connectivity to the two core DoD land management concerns—legal compliance and viability of the military mission—and to the other conditions of DoD's current natural and cultural resource management program highlighted in Figure 10. Of special concern is the extent to which new requirements will also be governed by the relatively quiescent political process described in Figures 7 and 10.

First, we address the effect of ecosystem management on the DoD role. Second, we assess the effects of recent DoD setbacks in attempting to access extended lands for military mission use.

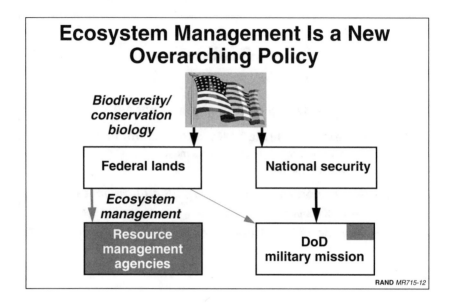

Figure 12

NEW SCIENCE, POLICIES, AND PROBLEMS

A significant new factor is the Clinton administration's overarching policy of ecosystem management. The policy is a response to growing concerns about habitat fragmentation and the loss of biodiversity. There is a scientific near-consensus on the importance of biodiversity although the basis for this consensus is, in the authors' judgment, less specific than that for other scientific principles.[24] A new science, conservation biology, has emerged to support planning for biodiversity conservation, which appears to be valued by a large segment of U.S. society. As illustrated in Figure 12, which is similar to the model presented in Figure 6, ecosystem management is a pol-

---

[24]Reasons cited for the importance of biodiversity generally include (1) the aesthetic value of biodiversity, (2) the potential application of chemical compounds derived from living things, and (3) the inherent complexity of the earth's biological relationships, implying a strong need not to eradicate species and processes whose role we do not fully understand.

icy that has emerged as a result of core citizen and scientific values and the political process for managing federal lands.

As a federal land manager, DoD was included in ecosystem management policy, and top-level DoD political leadership was quick to adopt the framework in DoD policy. However, the institution responds with greater ease to specific enforceable natural resource statutes than to general overarching natural resource policy. This policy asks agencies to manage along ecosystem rather than political boundaries, which may appear to some in DoD to go beyond the objectives of ecological compliance and mission viability. As such, the policy may appear as a broad executive mandate that actually works against DoD's core military concerns.

Conservation Biology

Before discussing the policy of ecosystem management, we explore the emerging science of conservation biology, on which the policy is partly based. This science is multidisciplinary, combining traditional ecology, wildlife biology, meteorology, geology, and other fields, to provide the scientific underpinnings for conservation and enhancement of biodiversity. It reflects the scientific view about the importance of biodiversity. As such, the thrust of conservation biology is to understand the effects of both human-induced and natural events on biodiversity and to develop strategies to mitigate for those effects.

Conservation biology provides the scientific underpinnings for supporting biodiversity on damaged or fragmented habitats. It calls for management across ecological boundaries and expresses the need even for small landholders to understand the processes governing large ecosystems. This "world view" is critical when much of the larger ecosystem has been destroyed. In such cases, the remaining small landholders may need to actively simulate the larger ecosystem processes to conserve biodiversity.[25]

---

[25]See G. Meffe and C. Carroll, *Principles of Conservation Biology*, Sinauer Associates, Inc., 1994, for a thorough textbook presentation of this emerging science and discussions of the species-area relationship.

Ecosystem Management

Conservation biology is only about 15–20 years old and still must cope with uncertainties about the definition of biodiversity, how to measure it, and why it is a critical measure. Therefore, any resource management policy based on conservation biology will be underdeveloped. The Clinton administration's policy of ecosystem management represents perhaps the most ambitious attempt to apply aspects of conservation biology. This policy calls for all agencies to look beyond their borders and contribute to the solution of environmental problems at an ecosystem level.[26] The policy emerged as a recommendation of the September 1993 National Performance Review. A White House Interagency Ecosystem Management Task Force was formed and directed to report on seven ecosystem management initiatives and methods of institutionalizing ecosystem management into federal policy.

There are widely different definitions of ecosystem management. The most common element seems to be the concept of ecological boundaries. Beyond this principle, there is a wide variety of goals and approaches. To the extent that the conservation of biodiversity is a goal, ecosystem management becomes applied conservation biology. However, it is also possible to manage entire ecosystems with highly utilitarian goals and priority systems. For example, the timber yield of a forest might well be enhanced by management along ecological rather than political boundaries.

Each major federal agency has its own slight variations of ecosystem management.[27] The Clinton administration's policy is based on a variety of sources and places a strong emphasis on conserving biodiversity. However, the policy is more typically explained as a proactive approach to "avoid the train wrecks"—the problems that occur when individual landholders try to solve problems without

---

[26]An August 8, 1994, memorandum from the Deputy Undersecretary of Defense (Environmental Security) states, "I want to ensure that ecosystem management becomes the basis for future management of DoD lands and waters." Detailed guidance entitled "Department of Defense Ecosystem Management Principles" is attached with instructions regarding the priority of biodiversity, ecological boundaries, etc.

[27]See Congressional Research Service, *Ecosystem Management and Federal Agencies*, Report # 94-339-ENR, 19 April 1994.

regard to overall ecosystem processes. However, almost all of the seven ecosystem initiatives launched by the administration were in response to specific "train wrecks." For example, the conflict over the spotted owl in the Pacific Northwest, the effects of the Valdez oil spill in the Prince William Sound, and the problems of water quality and quantity in South Florida were well-publicized "train wrecks" prior to the administration's new approach.

Even though the administration's version of ecosystem management incorporates many of the principles of conservation biology, it also gives consideration to utilitarian values. The nine goals listed in the interagency committee's draft report reflect both conservation and utilitarian values: (1) development of a shared vision of ecosystem health that includes human activity, (2) coordinated approaches among land holders, (3) maintenance of biological diversity, (4) sustainment of socioeconomic values, (5) respecting private property rights, (6) recognizing the dynamic nature of ecosystems, (7) use of adaptive management, (8) integration of the best scientific knowledge, and (9) establishment of baseline measurements of ecosystem health. Goals 3, 6, and 7 above are derivatives from conservation biology, with item 6 reflecting a key hypothesis of the new science. Goals 4 and 5 represent other values, requiring different measures from those for the utilitarian or conservation approach.

Although the Clinton administration's policy for ecosystem management (as well as that of the individual agencies) cannot be interpreted as applied conservation biology, it nonetheless utilizes the principles of this new science as a foundation of policy. These principles suggest that DoD needs to cooperate with other agencies and to engage in ecological concerns and the associated policy issues beyond the boundaries of its bases if it is to be a participant in ecosystem management.

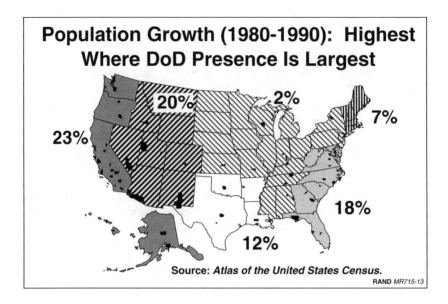

Figure 13

As a prelude to further discussion of ecosystem management, we note that concern about biodiversity has been driven by population growth, the associated suburbanization, and loss of habitat. Figure 13 illustrates percentages of population growth in the United States in the 1980s and highlights a central reason why ecosystem management may potentially relate to the core concerns of legal compliance and military training. Population growth—and the associated loss of habitat and biodiversity—has been greatest in those states that contain significant habitat reserves and open space. These are also the regions where the DoD has most of its installations. DoD has an extensive presence in the Rocky Mountain West, the far West, and the Southeast.

In the Rocky Mountain West, the percentage of population growth was large, but given the low base population in 1980, absolute population growth still lagged the other high-growth areas. The distinction between percentage of and absolute population growth is important for DoD and will become more transparent in the following text.

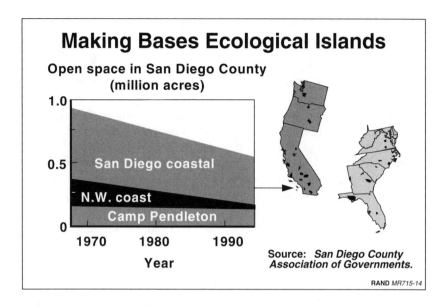

Figure 14

ECOLOGICAL ISLANDS

One result of absolute population growth—often in the Southeast and far West—is highlighted in Figure 14. Many bases are becoming "ecological islands" as a result of suburban encroachment. These "islands" may in some cases represent the only large remaining patches of original habitat in the region. Federal lands, even when there is a history of commodity production, typically retain more of the original ecosystems than lands used for urban and suburban development. As indicated in Figure 4, the only federal lands in many regions are managed by DoD. This is less true in the Rocky Mountain West, where DoD holdings are often bordered by far larger BLM holdings.

Camp Pendleton is perhaps the most extreme example of a military ecological island. The camp lies on the Southern California Coast on the northern edge of San Diego County and just south of Orange County, two of the fastest growing counties in California. The town of San Clemente abuts against the camp's northern border.

Oceanside and the other towns of northwestern San Diego County border the base to the south.

The pace of suburban sprawl is illustrated in Figure 14, which shows the open space in San Diego County as measured by the County Association of Governments (SANDAG).[28] Open space at Camp Pendleton is essentially unchanged over two decades but is disappearing from the county's northwest planning zone surrounding Camp Pendleton. Open space in the coastal region as a whole has also declined dramatically. Of greater significance, although not specifically detailed in Figure 14, is the disappearance of large patches of open space (excluding Camp Pendleton) where the coastal sage habitat occurs. Camp Pendleton is the only significant break in coastal development between Los Angeles and San Diego.

The problem at Camp Pendleton may be the most dramatic in the nation, but it is not unique. Numerous bases in the Southeast, such as Forts Bragg, Stewart, Polk, and Jackson, and Eglin Air Force Base, have become part of the last remaining habitat for the red cockaded woodpecker and the old-growth long-leaf pine ecosystem, an ecosystem that once stretched continuously from Eastern Texas to Southern Pennsylvania. Fort Lewis is sandwiched between Tacoma and Olympia, both of which are pressured by growth from Seattle. Bases near Washington D.C., such as Fort Belvoir, face similar external pressures.

CONSERVATION BIOLOGY, LEGAL COMPLIANCE, AND THE MILITARY MISSION

Conservation biology (and the associated policy of ecosystem management) is the science of managing for biodiversity on fragmented habitats. As such it may be more relevant to DoD than to any other federal agency. It may offer scientific principles and approaches for DoD natural resource management.

---

[28]SANDAG has not collected a consistent set of data over 30 years, so the data in Figure 14 represent our efforts to harmonize data from different planning reports measuring open space for different regions of the county. See *Land Use in the San Diego Region*, SANDAG INFO, January–February, 1993, for the type of information gathered.

Difficulty lies in the lack of complete overlap between biological diversity and the compelling DoD rationales of compliance and military training. Biodiversity is valued by the scientific community and large segments of society, but there are no statutes mandating its conservation. While to some the Endangered Species Act may well imply a biodiversity goal, even many of its strongest supporters acknowledge that its orientation is to provide single-species protection.

In the following charts, we expand the case study of Camp Pendleton to further examine the connectivity between ecosystem management and the twin DoD legal goals of compliance and mission viability. We also examine the feasibility of implementing ecosystem management in DoD given programmatic limitations.

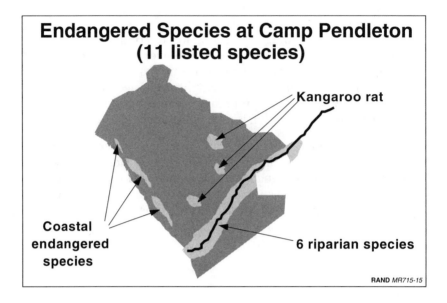

Figure 15

Figure 15 illustrates a direct relationship between ecological islands and DoD's compliance obligations and military training goals. Camp Pendleton is now the home of 11 species listed under the Endangered Species Act.[29] Several of these endangered species are dependent on the riparian habitat along the Santa Marguerita River—Southern California's only example of a river that has not been significantly altered by dams or riverbed improvement. The re-

---

[29]These include (1) California least tern, (2) least bell's vireo, (3) light-footed clapper rail, (4) brown pelican, (5) peregrine falcon, (6) California gnatcatcher, (7) western snowy plover, (8) Stephen's kangaroo rat, (9) tidewater goby, (10) riverside fairy shrimp, and (11) San Diego button-celery. Perhaps of greatest significance is the least bell's vireo, of which the U.S. Fish and Wildlife Service estimates that 348 territorial males have been observed at Camp Pendleton—238 on the Santa Marguerita River alone. *Status of Least Bell's Vireo and Southwestern Willow Flycatcher on Camp Pendleton Marine Corps Base, California in 1994*, U.S. Fish and Wildlife Service, April 1995. One biologist from the Kern River Research Center estimates this to be as much as 30 percent of the known population. The Carlsbad Office of the U.S. Fish and Wildlife Service estimates the figure could even be as high as 50 percent of the known population. Twenty years ago, estimates were less reliable, but the camp may have had as little as 5 percent of the total known population.

sulting importance of conservation of this habitat has meant the virtual exclusion of river-crossing in military training activities and has magnified difficulties in finding locations for helicopter touchdowns. Amphibious landing locations at the beach are also limited, and there are further restrictions due to the presence of the Stephen's kangaroo rat. Special care has to be taken to ensure that weapons firing does not create fires that will lead to cataclysmic destruction of these habitats.

In addition to some restrictions on military training, almost all activities at the base have been made more problematic. Construction, recreation, and all other activities of the 37,000 active Marines, 2,600 reservists, and 3,500 civilian employees should involve coordination with natural resource experts to ensure that endangered species are not affected. Such coordination does not always occur.

The management difficulties resulting from this type of island phenomena are, in the immediate sense, linked to the Endangered Species Act, which is under congressional review. The Carlsbad Office of the Fish and Wildlife Service is located only a few miles from the camp and pays close attention to camp activities. Should there be a softening of the act, many restrictions at Camp Pendleton could ease. However, Camp Pendleton is located in one of the most environmentally conscious regions of the world, and it seems likely that the State of California would find or create legal hurdles to ensure that the camp's rare habitat is protected. In general, the destruction of surrounding habitats has made Camp Pendleton a subject of increasing interest for regulatory attention. Oscillations in the level of attention are likely to occur, but the continued disappearance of surrounding habitats will, in the long run, likely generate increasing interest in Camp Pendleton's ecology among those concerned with both the scientific and regulatory aspects of ecosystems.

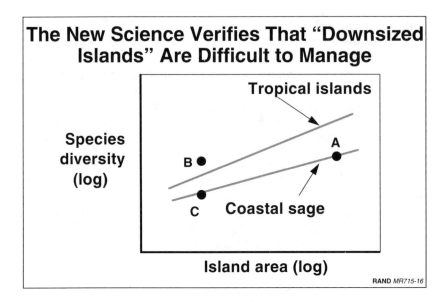

Figure 16

In the preceding discussion, we argued that there is a general relationship between DoD's legal compliance problems and the ecological island phenomenon. Figure 16 amplifies this discussion, indicating additional reasons why DoD should remain sensitive to developments in conservation biology and ecosystem management.

Figure 16 portrays the species-area curve that is a central empirical observation of conservation biology. The curve, sometimes referred to as the "theory of island biogeography," implies that the island phenomenon not only makes Camp Pendleton's ecology more valuable, but also makes management more difficult.[30] Once-satisfactory practices may no longer meet the requirements for sustaining a shrunken ecosystem. Bases located in regions experiencing rapid ecological change have a strong interest in regional habitat planning and in adopting internal management approaches to offset the future impact of continued degradation of surrounding habitats.

---

[30]See Meffe and Carroll, 1994, for a thorough discussion of the species-area relationship.

THE SPECIES-AREA CURVE

The species diversity–island area relationship (or species-area relationship) has been formulated from observations of islands of differing sizes located in similar climate regions and with similar coarse habitat characteristics. As noted in Figure 16, different categories of islands fall on different curves. The species-area relationship has been observed for several hundred years but in recent decades has been bolstered by strong empirical evidence and broad scientific consensus, though still falling short of scientific law. The specific determinants of the relationship have not been precisely defined because there is no obvious means of gaining control over the necessary processes since only naturally occurring habitats are available for testing. Islands that are close together form the best hope of controlling for climate distinctions but have increased potential for species migration and a corresponding dampening of the area effect.

While there is still no complete understanding of the underlying cause(s) of the relationship, three factors are often cited. First, and perhaps most critical, is that larger areas are less vulnerable to cataclysmic events that cause extinctions. For example, species on a large island are more likely to find places to hide from fire than those on a smaller island. Secondly, some species—most notably large carnivores—simply require larger habitats for survival. Finally, conservation biology has highlighted the "microscopic" variability that underlies coarse pictures of habitat. This "landscape" within a habitat is highly dynamic and may vary with time and processes such as wind, fire, rain, etc. Larger islands will inherently contain more of this diversity and, hence, the potential for more species. On small islands, the dynamic nature of the landscape implies that certain landscape patterns will disappear as a result of external processes.

This discussion points to the fundamental way in which conservation biology has reshaped our understanding of nature. The "classical" description of nature, sometimes referred to as the "balance of nature" concept, portrayed nature as stable and evolving toward a final climax state.[31] In this paradigm, a conservation goal

---

[31]These terms and description are adapted from *Conservation Biology: The Theory and Practice of Nature Conservation Preservation and Management*, P. Fiedler and S. Jain, eds., Chapman and Hall, 1993. In particular Chapter 4, "The New Paradigm in

was thought to be achievable by simply setting aside a patch of land and allowing that patch to reach ecological climax. However, extinctions on well-protected reserves, caused by the impact of dynamic external processes, invalidated this perspective and led to an hypothesis based on the "flux of nature." In this more modern view, dynamic processes affect the status of a particular patch of ground. Attempting to achieve a conservation goal on a small patch of what was once a larger ecosystem requires replication of the larger ecosystem processes and their effects. Rather than focusing on land management and preservation, the new paradigm points to management of dynamic processes. It implies the need for managers to actively simulate necessary processes which have disappeared because of the destruction of surrounding habitats.

APPLICATION TO A MILITARY BASE

Application of the area-species curve to continental conditions is fraught with uncertainty since the potential for species migration is different than that on true islands.[32] Identification of "island boundaries" is subjective even in the dramatic case of Camp Pendleton, where coastal sage gives way to suburbs over short distances. Nevertheless, the species-area relationship does capture some basic trends in refuges surrounded by suburbs or urban development.

The application to military bases is illustrated by the path A-B-C in Figure 16. At one time, Camp Pendleton and the surrounding coastal sage habitat could be represented by point A, a large area containing numerous indigenous and unique species. Rapid habitat destruction caused by suburbanization (rapid relative to any natural species extinction processes) moved the base to point B, a smaller "island" still

---

Ecology . . ." provides an excellent and easy-to-understand summary of the recent revolution in the scientific understanding of nature.

[32]For a criticism of application of the theory of island biogeography to the mainland, see *Habitat Conservation Planning: Endangered Species and Urban Growth*, T. Beatley, University of Texas Press, 1994. Another critical assessment can be found in "Extinction: Are Ecologists Crying Wolf?" *Science*, Vol. 243, p. 736, August 16, 1991. While these critiques attack detailed aspects of the species-area relationship and the application to mainland settings, they do not seem to attack the general existence of a relationship between area and diversity.

containing roughly the same biodiversity as the larger one. Random natural disturbances—which would not be severe enough to eradicate species from the original large ecosystem—will now have a more destructive effect on the small "island" and bring the base toward point C. Many of the species threatened by these natural processes are inevitably listed in the Endangered Species Act.

Camp Pendleton is now at point B. Rapid suburbanization has reduced "island area," random natural processes will cause extinctions, and there is virtually no opportunity for repopulation from nearby habitats. To counter that tendency, resource managers must take active steps that simulate the processes and behavior of larger "islands." One activity is to ensure the appropriate fire regime. At Camp Pendleton, this means rapid and intense fire suppression since the region can be quite dry and military activities exacerbate the problem by causing frequent fires. A severe fire could wipe out much of the riparian habitat along the Santa Marguerita River. If other off-base riparian habitats existed, a cataclysmic fire might be tolerable because of the potential for repopulation.

Fort Bragg is at a similar, but perhaps less critical, point on a species-area curve. However, the prescription for active management is quite different. A fire regime that mimics the natural and frequent fire setting processes in the long-leaf pine ecosystem is required. But due to the reduced size of the ecosystem, these fires must be controlled to avoid the adverse effects on old pine trees that could have been tolerated in a larger pine forest.

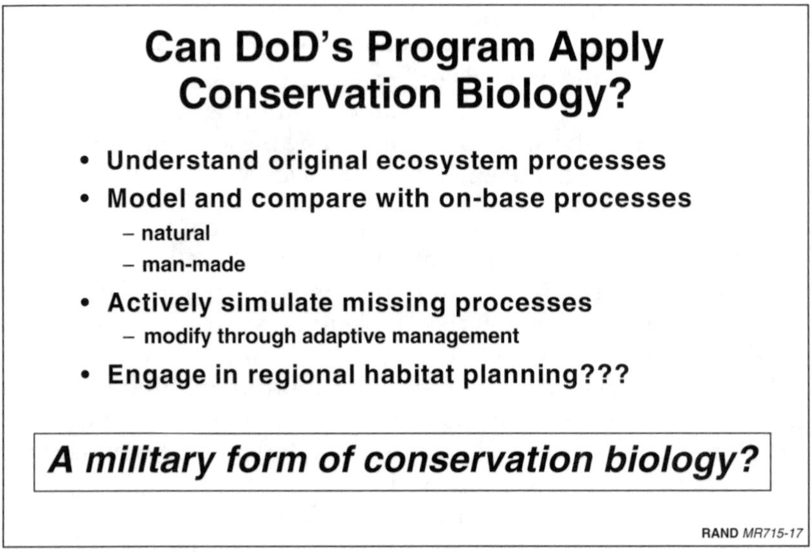

Can DoD's Program Apply Conservation Biology?

- **Understand original ecosystem processes**
- **Model and compare with on-base processes**
  - natural
  - man-made
- **Actively simulate missing processes**
  - modify through adaptive management
- **Engage in regional habitat planning???**

A military form of conservation biology?

RAND *MR715-17*

Figure 17

THE REQUIREMENTS

We have discussed previously why ecosystem management and conservation biology are of critical interest to bases. Conservation biology is the science of conserving biodiversity on fragmented habitats and therefore has a long-term, but incomplete, relationship to DoD's core goals of legal compliance and mission viability. Since it is the only scientific framework for analysis of DoD's "island" problem, DoD should seek to understand its implications and incorporate relevant components in the DoD land management program. Figure 17 summarizes some of these implications and poses a question of whether a modified "military conservation biology" could be developed that is consistent with DoD's programmatic constraints.

A central implication is the need to employ active management techniques for "island-like" bases. Selecting the correct approaches will require analysis of all the natural processes that led to formation of the original larger ecosystem, followed by analysis of the natural and human processes occurring within the military base. This analysis would then be followed by active management to address distinctions between what is occurring and what is required. Constant reevaluation (adaptive management) will be required since the underlying science is subject to significant uncertainty.

Finally, the policy implications of the science point to the need for active DoD participation in off-base environmental affairs. Bases should take an interest in regional habitats and in ensuring that lands off-base are reserved for habitat protection. Failure to preserve habitat off-base will eventually increase the management burden on-base. Several levels of actions are possible, including remaining sensitive to the possibility of off-site mitigation, analysis of off-base habitat destruction trends, and active participation in the growing number of regions conducting habitat planning. However, in addition to simply ensuring that the maximum amount of off-base habitat is preserved, conservation biology has also led to predictions that the shape of reserves and their connectivity can have important implications.

THE CONSTRAINTS

Unfortunately, Camp Pendleton and virtually every other DoD installation are not in a position to adopt this approach. Their programs must cope with immediate ESA and other compliance issues, and there is little time or staff available for strategic planning involving internal or external affairs. The diverse military tenants at Camp Pendleton and the partial isolation of the environmental program implies that it would be almost impossible to carefully document all the processes occurring at the base and to link them to the base ecology.[33] At Camp Pendleton, the recently successful innovative attempt to develop a multispecies ESA consultation with the Fish and Wildlife Service for the riparian habitat stretched staff resources and

---

[33]The diverse tenants at Camp Pendleton include the 1st Marine Expeditionary Force, the Marine Corps Recruit Depot, the Naval Hospital, Marine Corps Tactical, state parks, agricultural and other leases, and a wide range of visiting units. See *Marine Corps Base Camp Pendleton*, Directory and Guide, 1994, for a complete listing of units at Camp Pendleton.

at times seemed to be more ambitious and creative than required by cautious regulators.[34]

Perhaps most significant, DoD's nature land cultural resource program does not have the tradition for engaging in off-base environmental issues and the regional habitat planning implied by conservation biology. The implications of this inward-looking focus are discussed in Figure 18.

MILITARY CONSERVATION BIOLOGY?

Application of many aspects of conservation biology to military bases seems beyond the practical concerns of limited staffing, the priority of immediate legal compliance issues, the inability of bases to truly manage beyond base boundaries (as discussed below), and even at times the difficulty in developing a complete picture of land use at a base. Nevertheless, the multispecies consultation at Camp Pendleton is an example of an effort that moves in the direction of conservation biology. It integrates numerous installation activities and develops a broad-based measure of environmental effects (as measured by the status of six species). It also satisfies an immediate compliance obligation.

This suggests that it may be possible to blend the principles of conservation biology with immediate requirements. Despite the scientific goal of management along ecological boundaries, delineation of such boundaries always contains ambiguity and leaves the need to model the physical and biological flows across such lines. Moreover, several existing ecosystem initiatives utilizing ecological boundaries have been criticized for being too large and too politically complex to

---

[34]The outline for a multispecies Section VII consultation was presented in briefing form to the Carlsbad Office of the U.S. Fish and Wildlife Service on July 28, 1994. It involved six listed species and comprehensive uses of the riparian habitat, including military training, flood control, facilities maintenance, helicopter landings, and other construction activities. It took more than a year of intense negotiations and planning to finally reach agreement. Biological Opinion 1-6-95-F-02, "Programmatic Activities and Conservation Plans in Riparian and Estuarine/Beach Ecosystems on Marine Base, Camp Pendleton," U.S. Fish and Wildlife Service, October 30, 1995.

test these new management principles.[35] The size of many military bases and the unity of command may make them excellent laboratories to advance application of conservation biology while helping installations with both short- and long-term management challenges.[36]

We conclude that there may be a form of ecosystem management that can take place within the boundaries of a military installation. It would be desirable to conduct a pilot examination of the requirements for managing a base using the principles of conservation biology. The outcome could then be compared with compliance obligations and the tasks and plans required for compliance that are by necessity of top priority for natural resource staff. It might then be possible to adapt mandated activities so that they fulfill obligations while helping build a more proactive approach toward managing a fragmented ecosystem.

We should note that during the latter half of 1995, DoD and The Keystone Center convened a dialogue to move in the direction highlighted above. The dialogue faced the dilemma of trying to match programmatic constraints with scientific principles and the differing perspectives of individuals charged with fulfilling different responsibilities. The pilot examination mentioned above would seem a logical continuation of the dialogue.[37]

---

[35]See United States General Accounting Office, *ECOSYSTEM MANAGEMENT Additional Actions Needed to Adequately Test a Promising Approach*, GAO/RCED-94-111, August 1994.

[36]One example of this management approach can be found in *Natural Resources Management Plan, Eglin Air Force Base 1993–1997*, Air Force Development Test Center, Eglin AFB, Fl. The Eglin plan incorporates many of the principles of conservation biology; however, Eglin does not have the close coupling of military mission and environment that provides the most stressful management challenges.

[37]See *Keystone Center Policy Dialogue on Department of Defense (DoD) Biodiversity Final Report (DRAFT)*, November 8, 1995.

Regional Habitat Planning, but . . .

- **Mojave shows the problems:**
  - inward-looking bases/services
  - local and regional laws/alliances
  - base histories
- **Pendleton the risks:**
  - weak politically
  - few off-base options
- **Bragg the promise?**
  - important regional player
  - bad history corrected
- **Yakima the future?**
  - proactive regional studies

RAND *MR715-18*

Figure 18

The potential benefits of ecosystem management for DoD were discussed in the context of Figure 17. In general, the failure to look outward may make resource management on existing bases more difficult. Studying processes outside base boundaries also allows for the design of a proactive management strategy within a base. The difficulty, and fear within DoD, is the potential diversion of limited resources and personnel away from core issues toward a broader set of regional concerns. Thus, DoD is faced with the question of when and how to engage in off-base issues and to what extent it should build capabilities to do so.

As a result of the Clinton administration policy and other events, a number of bases have engaged in regional habitat planning or broader ecosystem management (some examples are given in Figure 18). Even though DoD bases may have a general interest in regional habitat planning and broad-based ecosystem management, for these efforts to be considered productive for DoD they should serve DoD's central resource management concern, which is to reduce the pace at which the "island effect" is occurring. The outcome of engagement in regional habitat planning is not always beneficial; and timing is very important.   In addition to strategic planning for ecological issues, the cases illustrate that DoD bases require additional capabilities in policy and political analysis to determine the base's most productive role in regional habitat planning.[38]   This need is illustrated below with four examples in which DoD has attempted to engage in regional ecosystem planning.

THE MOJAVE DESERT ECOSYSTEM MANAGEMENT INITIATIVE

Evolution of the Initiative

Most prominent among DoD's efforts to examine ecological roles beyond base boundaries has been the Mojave Desert Ecosystem Management Initiative.   The origins of the initiative have not been formally documented except by internal memos between the Office of Environmental Policy (OEP) and DoD.   DoD was apparently asked by the White House to lead an ecosystem management initiative similar to those ongoing in other parts of the country.   As such, it originated from the White House policy for managing federal lands rather than from military concerns.

Initially, two ecosystem options for a DoD-led initiative, the Great Plains and the Upper Rio Grande, were suggested by the OEP.   The DoD countered by proposing the longleaf pine ecosystem, the big island of Hawaii, and the Mojave.   The Mojave was chosen because DoD has four critical installations in the Western Mojave (Fort Irwin, China Lake Naval Weapons Testing Center, Edwards Air Force Base, and 29 Palms Marine Combat Center) and several bases at the edge or just beyond the Mojave (Nellis Air Force Base and the Chocolate Mountains Gunnery Range).   Moreover, the Army has long had the goal of expanding Fort Irwin—the home of the National Training Center and arguably the Army's single most critical installation.

---

[38]Guidance for Army regulation AR-420-74 states,

> To the greatest extent practicable, installation commanders and Army natural resource planners and managers at all levels will develop and implement policies and strategies to assist, in cooperation with other landowners, in achieving the following objectives. . . .

The guidance then goes on to list objectives such as maintenance of viable species populations, genetic variability, ecosystems, etc.

What followed in attempting to implement the Mojave initiative was an indication of the extent to which DoD's program had developed an inward-looking orientation and its difficulty in considering problems beyond base boundaries. It is also an indication that to be useful, a broad-based policy of ecosystem management must be carefully tailored to the ecological and political conditions surrounding an installation. However, the difficulties in communicating natural resource issues up and down the chain of command made this extremely difficult in the Mojave.

Subsequent to the announcement of the initiative, it quickly became clear that the DoD, the White House, and DoI headquarters had not properly gauged the willingness of the actors in the region to accept DoD as a leader and organizer of a regional ecosystem initiative. The BLM is the dominant landholder in the region and has a far longer history of regional activity. It also had its own ongoing, smaller-scale ecosystem planning efforts, in which the DoD bases had previously declined to participate. More important, with an organizational structure more like that of the USFS, BLM had a far greater grasp of the region's ecology and the impact of human activities on the region than did DoD. As a result, BLM resisted DoD's efforts to conclude a memorandum of understanding (MOU) on a Mojave-wide ecosystem management initiative.

Equally significant was the lack of interest by the military services and even some of the natural resource personnel at installations. Since natural resources offices were overwhelmed by the chronic problem of small staffs dealing with on-base problems, the services saw no need for an initiative that was at least partially designed to enhance policy for all federal lands rather than DoD lands specifically. They resisted taking leadership and that role was passed to the Los Angeles district of the Army Corps of Engineers. Notably, the corps' Los Angeles district is not a desert land manager but an engineering support office primarily concerned with operation of the Los Angeles flood control system and dredging at the harbor. With no DoD desert land manager willing to lead and poor relations between the Army Corps and the other federal agencies, resistance to cooperation grew.[39] Ultimately, DoD agreed to a more balanced role with the BLM and to change the initiative from the Mojave to the California desert; boundaries that had less ecological meaning but corresponded to BLM's traditional administrative boundaries. This violated one of the fundamental principles of ecosystem management, which is to manage for ecological rather than political boundaries. The new boundaries did, however, correspond closely to the boundaries of the California Desert Protection Act of 1994. As part of the compromise, DoD also agreed to sign the California Biodiversity Agreement, an agreement that BLM had already signed and viewed as an integral part of ecological planning in the desert.

The details of the ensuing events are less clear, but at this point, the military services began to stiffen resistance and may have made their objections known to members of Congress. A critical stumbling block was the "fine print" in the California Biodiversity Agreement, which called for focusing biodiversity conservation efforts on federal lands as a trade-off to permit private development on nonfederal lands. Since the California Biodiversity Agreement is clearly aimed at supporting private development interests in the state, the services became concerned that it was not in DoD's interest to agree to such principles. The Marine Corps seemed to voice the greatest concerns and much of its anxiety may have been due to the potential implications for Camp Pendleton, rather than to fear that 29 Palms, a remote desert facility, would become an ecological reserve. The DoD developed two alternative modifications to the California Biodiversity Agreement, but before they could be formally negotiated, the initiative was abandoned as political controversy increased.

The objections of the services reached the new Congress, which was examining DoD environmental programs with new vigor and paying particular attention to activities that did not seem to correspond to traditional DoD interests. Jerry Lewis, the local congressman, documented his objections in a letter to DoD, the state of California, and the BLM. The DoD abandoned efforts to conclude a MOU with DoI

---

[39]The Army Corps put forth an original plan whose limited distribution and maps caused great anger and frustration in DoI, where it was perceived as a DoD plan for a "desert takeover." It included plans for eventual expansion of the initiative. *Mojave-Sonoran Ecosystem Management Initiative*, Los Angeles District, South Pacific Division, U.S. Army Corps of Engineers, undated.

and lowered the political profile of the initiative. Washington involvement was limited to a coordination role in the office of the Army's Director of Environmental Programs, and Fort Irwin's natural resource office became the local leader.[40] Fort Irwin then applied for Legacy funds for a project titled, "Mojave Ecosystem Inventory and Data Bank Cooperative." The proposal, which calls for a broad-based data-gathering effort across the Mojave (and potentially the California Desert), seemed to satisfy the requirements for an initiative but had little relationship to the all-encompassing ecosystem assessments that were the original intention of White House policy. Data gathering is intended to occur throughout the far reaches of the Mojave with little specific focus on DoD installations. At the time of this report, $2.5 million in Legacy funds had been allocated for the project, though its connection to conservation goals on DoD lands is unclear. Nor does the data-gathering proposal, in our judgment, necessarily appear to address DoD needs. Instead, it aims at a broad-based and loosely focused data-gathering effort across the broad expanses of the Mojave or the California Desert.

Lessons for DoD Ecosystem Management

There are numerous lessons that DoD can take away from the difficulties in the Mojave Desert. It is clear that bases or services are either unaware of the scientific and demographic trends discussed above or simply do not have the incentives or internal resources to develop an outward-looking perspective. This may not be a critical factor in situations like the Mojave. Despite growth in desert cities, the four bases are not on the verge of becoming "ecological islands." The lack of an outward perspective, in combination with the absence of a natural resource chain of command with a regional orientation, may explain why headquarters was unaware of the "poison pill" in the California Biodiversity Agreement.[41] Headquarters was also

---

[40]In an April 7 letter to Congressman Jerry Lewis, Sherri Goodman, the Deputy Undersecretary of Defense (Environmental Security) asked,

> I would hope, however, that you would not object to the installation commanders and their staffs continuing to engage their DoI counterparts on issues critical to protecting current and future missions.

[41]Also indicative of the difficulty in communicating up and down the chain of command was the lack of awareness by the natural resource coordinator at Fort

unaware of both the history and substantive knowledge that senior leadership in the California BLM had acquired. There was also a headquarters' lack of awareness about earlier DoD unwillingness to participate in ecosystem planning in the Mojave Desert.

DoD's role as the largest federal land manager without a resource management mission implies that when dealing with other land managers DoD will inevitably be represented by lower-ranking employees than the land management agencies. In areas where there are extensive federal lands, DoD is unlikely to be the most knowledgeable federal landholder. Whereas the National Park Service may send the park superintendent to attend a planning meeting, a DoD base commander is unlikely to attend a meeting that is not focused on his primary mission and would generally have a less substantive knowledge of resource management issues than his or her counterpart in a land management agency. More typically, DoD will be represented by the civilian environmental coordinator or head of the natural resource office. In the Mojave, this disparity in cooperative authority further exacerbated BLM's frustration.

More generally and more significantly, the timing and location of the DoD leadership role were poorly calculated. As noted above, the four major bases in the West Mojave are not in danger of falling victim to the problems of loss of surrounding habitat. Growth in the desert cities of Victorville, Lancaster, and Barstow has been dramatic and has created some regional ecological problems, such as supporting ravens that feed on the eggs of the threatened desert tortoise. Nevertheless, DoD bases in the Mojave are not on the verge of becoming ecological islands. Even though the bases contain unusual and valued resources, they do not play a decisive role in the regional ecology.

Nevertheless, the fragility of the desert tortoise population, the "poison pill" in the California Biodiversity Agreement, and the changing population growth patterns in the California desert do make it important for the four West Mojave bases to understand how

---

Irwin—the lead DoD operational representative—that agreement had been reached in Washington to shift the boundaries of the initiative from the Mojave to the California Desert. It was only through an informal meeting with two of the authors of this report that the Fort Irwin coordinator became aware of the change.

processes and events outside their boundaries may ultimately affect ecological management at the bases. At this time, it appears that the appropriate step is for each base to conduct base-centered strategic planning studies in an effort to identify future challenges. These studies might include a significant component of "military conservation biology" as discussed in the preceding two figures. Most important, by base-centered we mean a focus on internal base issues, more emphasis on adjacent lands and less on lands in the distant East Mojave, as envisioned in the original initiative. Rather than lead a broad-based data-gathering effort across the Mojave, DoD should use its $2.5 million investment to better identify which regional issues and trends will affect management of the four bases in the West Mojave. A DoD ecosystem management program in the Mojave may serve DoD interests, but given its history and role in the region, this will be true only if such an initiative is centered tightly around the four bases.[42]

CAMP PENDLETON

The other case studies highlighted in Figure 18 provide similar lessons regarding timing and the potential DoD role. Camp Pendleton is not now, nor has it ever been, an active participant in several well-publicized San Diego County habitat planning initiatives. Even though the base has for many years had an interest in the creation of off-base habitats, it is doubtful that early or enthusiastic participation would have altered developments in the region. The base has little political voice in this highly populated region, especially in comparison with the strength of the suburban development interests that dominated Orange and San Diego County politics throughout the 1970s and 1980s. It is possible that the outcome of participation may have been to attract more attention to the base as a potential "dumping ground" for endangered species. Currently,

---

[42]At a February 2, 1994, meeting at Fort Irwin attended by DoD Deputy Undersecretary Goodman and DoI Assistant Secretary Frampton, one DoD official presented a handout entitled "DoD-DoI Ecosystem Management in California Desert." It portrayed the initiative at three tiers: (1) desert-wide, (2) bioregional, and (3) site-specific (installation level). The discussion above implies that DoD should focus on tier 3 ecosystem planning, extending it to include adjacent lands.

the same obstacles apply, and there are even fewer "off-base" options for habitats.

Despite a need to integrate Camp Pendleton's ecological management into a broader regional structure, it appears there are both physical and political limitations to such a strategy. Many of the principles of conservation biology for management of Camp Pendleton's resources are relevant, but it is unlikely that engagement in regional habitat planning will enhance the base's ability to manage the installation for military training.

FORT BRAGG

If Pendleton and Mojave illustrate the obstacles to regional participation and engagement, ironically the Army's most notorious story of ecological management may now provide a successful model. Even though this effort focused on the narrow issue of red cockaded woodpecker (RCW) management, there are several factors that have allowed Fort Bragg to engage in a limited but, so far, successful regional effort. Perhaps the most important factor has been the time and financial resources that the leadership of Fort Bragg have dedicated to reversing a troubled history. In a few short years, Fort Bragg has become a center of expertise for study of RCW recovery and has engaged regional private landholders in efforts to share scientific information and to plan for the survival of the species across the Sandhills habitat.[43] The results have culminated in Fort Bragg's efforts to acquire an additional 11,000 acres, which would provide additional flexibility for both military maneuvers and habitat recovery.

Perhaps most significant, the timing of Fort Bragg's regional engagement may be far more appropriate than that for the Mojave. Bragg now stands as the main, but not the only, component of a long-leaf pine ecological island. Bragg hosts about 60 percent of the cavity sites for the RCW and, therefore, is the single most important ecological site in the region. However, the situation has not yet evolved to the point where off-base options have disappeared.

---

[43]A symposium on regional habitat planning was held at Fort Bragg in the fall of 1992.

It should also be mentioned that Fort Bragg is located in an area of the country where there is traditionally strong support for the military, and the pressure for development, though having created an island effect for Bragg, is not as powerful as in Orange and San Diego counties. Finally, we should emphasize that Bragg's regional efforts are not connected to a broad-vision conservation biology or ecosystem management, but instead are oriented toward exploitation of a particular technical advantage to enhance its regional reputation and enjoy regulatory flexibility.

YAKIMA

If the situation at Bragg can be juxtaposed with Pendleton, then the situation at Yakima is perhaps analogous to the bases in the Mojave. Yakima having recently acquired an additional 55,000 acres, the law authorizing the expansion calls for Yakima to undertake a series of ecological studies to help understand the long-term impact of the new acquisition. Yakima, like the desert bases, is far from becoming an ecological island, and the studies appear to represent the type of strategic planning exercises we believe might be most appropriate for the four bases in the West Mojave.

There are two types of studies being conducted. One is internally oriented and seeks to develop a basic understanding of the interaction between the military mission and the base ecology. Natural resource workers at Yakima have portrayed the study on a large wiring diagram linking diverse military activities to diverse measures of ecological health.[44] More significantly, it represents an effort to understand the processes created by the military mission and their effects on potential conservation goals.

---

[44]The CNRMP or Comprehensive Natural Resource Management Plan divides the Yakima "landscape" into seven watersheds and eight ecological variables for each watershed. The impact of human activities—including the military mission—will then be estimated for each variable and integrated to provide a assessment of watershed and landscape health. The Columbia Plateau Shrub-Steppe Conservation Strategy Framework has the stated overall goal

> to develop a model conservation strategy outlining protection needs for the maintenance of biodiversity of the Yakima Training Center within the context of the Columbia Plateau Shrub-Steppe (CPSS) ecosystem (draft study summary received from Yakima Training Center).

In the second study, in conjunction with the Nature Conservancy, Yakima is seeking to characterize the role of the base in the regional ecology. As mentioned earlier, Yakima is not in the foreseeable future likely to suffer greatly from the "ecological island" effect. However, the baseline study should provide DoD with a better ability to see how emerging trends may, in the long run, lead to that condition. These two studies of differing scale would seem to be ideal models for a DoD Mojave Desert initiative and for advancing the concept of "military conservation biology" as discussed earlier. Each base could develop a detailed picture of how its mission and activities are affecting long-run conditions on the base. Similarly, each base in the Mojave could then attempt to determine how regional trends will affect the requirements for natural resource management on the base.

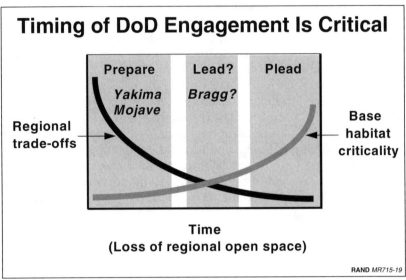

Figure 19

One of the more critical aspects of the preceding discussion can be summarized in the conceptual model illustrated in Figure 19. Although local political conditions have a significant impact, all four case studies indicate that timing of regional engagement is also critical. Figure 19 shows (notionally) that early engagement is desirable to ensure maximum potential for off-base habitats. A base's role in the politics of the regional ecology may become significant only when its decisions can strongly impact regional ecological trends. However, cooperating with federal, state, and local agencies in monitoring, planning, and strategy development can establish important working relationships and on-base capacity at any point in the evolution of the regional ecology.

Figure 19 also displays a notional assessment of the four preceding case studies. The figure suggests that the conditions at Fort Bragg may well be the best balance between influence and the disappearance of off-base options. However, Fort Bragg's future situation is unclear, given the fragile conditions in that ecosystem, which could easily lead Fort Bragg to "plead" rather than "lead." We again emphasize that this leadership is in a highly focused technical area related to RCW recovery. Given the presence of other large federal landholders in much of the west, and the presence of politically important nonfederal landholders in other parts of the country, there may be few true opportunities for DoD to exert leadership. Instead leadership may more typically mean active and frequent participation. This could occur at any point in the evolution of an ecosystem.

We conclude that DoD incorrectly judged the strategic position of the Mojave bases. There is no compelling reason for DoD to be a leader in the Mojave, even though off-base issues could ultimately provide threats to base ecological management. The bases would be well advised to increase their attention to these trends but are poorly positioned to lead a planning initiative. Therefore, we have placed "Mojave" in the "prepare" category, indicating these bases may undertake their own policy-relevant studies and monitor external ecological and political developments. DoD should also use the next few years to correct the reputations that plague some of the bases in the area. This would involve cooperation and discussions with local environmental agencies. In contrast, Yakima and Pendleton may have correctly gauged their influence and the available options. In Pendleton's case, local political dynamics appear to have been the main constraint on engagement and taking action in regional planning.

The Role of Planning and Analysis

1. **Prepare**
   - **Improve reputation**
   - **Acquire ability**
2. **Assess base role in regional ecology**
3. **Identify limitations of DoD influence**
4. **Assess benefits and risks of engagement**
5. **Decide to lead, plead, or participate**

RAND *MR715-20*

Figure 20

Figure 20 applies the discussions of the preceding chart to the question of determining planning and analysis strategies. DoD has a strong interest in regional habitat planning, ecosystem management, and conservation biology, but is vulnerable to a wide range of timing and political problems when engaging in regional efforts. It is not uncommon for DoD to be a small player in regional ecology politics. Only through DoD's deliberate assessment of its capability for analysis and planning can it safely determine its proper role in such processes.

The above cases indicate that bases first must attempt to correct any problems in their reputations and acquire the necessary understanding about regional habitat planning. This might include actions such as creating a community complaint hotline. Where such programs have been implemented, they have greatly boosted community relations.[45] Staffing with personnel familiar with natural and cultural

---

[45]Discussion of specific cases can be found in a Western Pacific Region Airspace Steering Committee Meeting memorandum, September 7, 1994.

resource management, the local ecology, and the local regulatory structure is critical at the outset. Staff must then determine the role of the base in the regional ecology and identify the opportunities and limitations of DoD influence in such processes. This strategic analysis should then lead to a decision to "lead" or "plead," i.e., determining a strategy for what actions and level of engagement are in DoD interests.

In conclusion, the president's policy of ecosystem management could provide a useful roadmap for DoD's land management program. However, DoD's unique resource management role implies that its program needs to be "customized" for a DoD context, applied with selectivity, and supported by the development of additional analytic capabilities within the current program.

Outline

- **DoD's role (25 million acres of bases)**

- **An expanded role? (*More than 25 million acres?*)**
    - biodiversity/ecosystem management
  ➤ - extended lands

- **A reduced role? (*Less than 25 million acres?*)**
    - utilitarian/development values

- **How does DoD balance countervailing forces?**

RAND *MR715-21*

Figure 21

In the following pages, we review the rationale for DoD engagement on extended lands and analyze the governance mechanism at work. By "extended lands," we mean the lands DoD sails near to, flies over, or seeks to use on a temporary or permanent basis. We will argue that governance of DoD engagement on extended lands differs in intensity and consistency from that within base boundaries. To best represent DoD core interests in the face of high uncertainty and scrutiny, additional capabilities for planning and strategic analysis will be needed to address military environmental issues on these lands. As with existing DoD lands, management of these lands will require selective DoD engagement with selected regional ecological issues.

Competition for Federal Lands

"From the view out the window of an F-15 aircraft overflying the western states, most of the land appears uninhabited. However every acre of federal land has been allocated to one or more user groups"

D. Mitchell, former chief counsel, Alaska Federation of Natives

RAND *MR715-22*

Figure 22

Figure 22 presents a comment by Donald Mitchell, the former chief counsel of the Alaska Federation of Natives. In combination with the map of federal lands in the West (the darkened areas on the map), the quote provides a concise summary of DoD's land use challenge on extended lands.

As noted earlier, the Rocky Mountain West has undergone a significant percentage of population growth but is still sparsely populated. Most of the growth has occurred in the area's urban centers, and by some measures the region is the most urbanized in the nation. As a result, there are still vast open spaces that represent potential areas for temporary, or more permanent, military training activities.

This demographic pattern provides the underlying rationale for Mitchell's portrayal. Despite population growth, much of the West remains just as empty as it was a few decades ago. However, population growth and urbanization has led to a proliferation of user groups and increased sophistication in accessing the political system. While the land may look empty, hunters, timber companies, river runners, wilderness backpackers, fly fishermen, pilots, off-road vehicle riders, environmentalists, miners, Native Americans, and others have all laid claim to use of federal land in the West.

Each of these groups has a trade association or nonprofit organization that employs lobbyists, attorneys, and professional staff to represent its members' interests on Capitol Hill, in the executive branch, and in the states where the relevant user groups are most prominent. For that reason, any DoD agency that seeks to make use of land not already under its administrative control (or even for new uses of airspace already under its administrative control) can expect that its request will be opposed by one or more user groups whose members have an interest in the same acreage. For example, a nonprofit, membership- and foundation-funded group known as the Rural Alliance for Military Accountability (RAMA) seeks to organize these disparate user groups when DoD initiatives emerge.

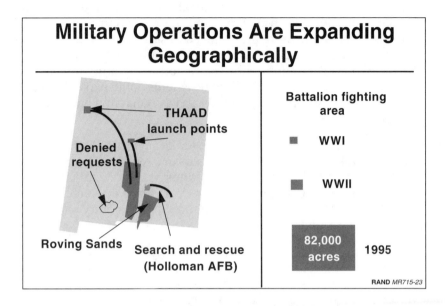

Figure 23

The challenge implied by the changing demographics of the West is magnified by the expanding scope of military operations. Figure 23 illustrates two representative examples of this expansion.

The right side of the figure illustrates the Army's understanding of the battle space required for a battalion at three separate points in history.[46] New weapons and tactics have expanded that space to approximately 82,000 acres from just a few thousand acres in the two world wars. Such numbers are consistent with a broad spectrum of changes in Army weapons systems and tactics. Similarly, the Air Force's need for airspace is also increasing. A World War II fighter required approximately a 5-nautical-mile maneuvering radius; to-

---

[46]Data provided by the Office of the Deputy Assistant Secretary of the Army (Occupational Health, Safety, and the Environment). The two sides of the figure are not to scale.

day's fighters require about 80 nautical miles.[47]   With deeper-draft vessels, naval impacts on estuaries and shorelines surrounding Naval bases are becoming more pronounced, resulting in the need for increased dredging near shorelines and harbors. Recent changes in Navy strategy also require more ships to be operating in coastline waters.[48] Finally, training area requirements could expand at some bases as the BRAC process proceeds and as remaining bases are utilized more intensively.

Drawn to a different scale, the left side of Figure 23 highlights the impact of these changing training needs in a region that would seem to offer DoD great freedom of operations; it has few urban centers and contains vast DoD land holdings.[49] Despite these characteristics, there seem to be an increasing number of military requests to utilize off-base lands in the area.

The two top arcs in Figure 23 represent missile test trajectories for the Theater High-Altitude Area Defense (THAAD) System. To obtain the required speeds and trajectories over the target intercept area on the two-million-acre White Sands test range, launches must take place well beyond the boundaries of the range. Current plans are to conduct launches from Fort Wingate, a closed Army depot in the northwest corner of New Mexico, and from a small private parcel about 40 miles north of White Sands that has been leased from private landholders for this purpose.

Holloman Air Force Base is in the process of requesting unlimited use of approximately 15–20 square mile areas in each of 5 BLM districts.[50] The requests are aimed at supporting requirements for expanded search and rescue training. At the time of this writing, only

---

[47]Commission on Base Realignment and Closure, as discussed in G. H. Siehl, *Natural Resource Issues in National Defense Programs,* Congressional Research Service Report for Congress, October 31, 1991.

[48]*Defense Environment Alert,* May 3, 1995, p. 29.

[49]Readers interested in gaining further perspective on the politics of land use in the West are referred to a novel entitled *Fire on the Mountain,* by Edward Abbey (New York: Avon Books, 1992). It describes the long history of strong resistance to military land acquisition and use in this region, even at a time when the land seemed like an endless resource.

[50]Memorandum from Holloman Air Force Base Deputy Base Civil Engineer to BLM Area Manager, Caballo Resource Area, February 28, 1995.

two districts had received this request and both had rejected it. FLPMA is specific about the role of military operations on BLM lands and is generally restrictive.[51]

Finally, the joint air defense exercise Roving Sands, which was expanded a few years ago, has also taken on increased geographical scope. The Army recently utilized part of the McGregor Range at Fort Bliss that had previously not typically been used for military training. McGregor Range is a 700,000 acre extension of Fort Bliss that is withdrawn public land requiring renewal in 2001 under the Military Lands Withdrawal Act of 1986. This first-time use apparently angered some hunting groups that utilize the land.[52] Also, as part of the expanded Roving Sands exercise, visiting units from Fort Bragg requested temporary use of BLM land outside the McGregor/Bliss complex, but the request was refused.[53]

These two examples are only illustrative cases but are representative of more intensive and expansive resource requirements for military training. We should, however, note that there is not necessarily a one-to-one correspondence between the span of operations and the need for more land and airspace. For Army missions one view is that small-unit training can be conducted within existing base bound-

---

[51]Section 302 of FLPMA limits use of public lands by the military to (1) withdrawals, (2) rights of way, (3) cooperative agreements for uses similar to nonmilitary uses permitted on those lands, and (4) some special provisions for Alaska. The BLM also allows casual use, defined as activities that are transient, with no or minimal environmental impacts. BLM requires that such "casual use" actions be coordinated with the Bureau. The only complete documentation of DoI policy is in a now expired (but still accurate) instruction memorandum from the Assistant Director, Land and Renewable Resources, Instruction Memorandum No. 91-283, May 21, 1991. It officially expired on September 30, 1993.

[52]The Army has the right to deny public access, see *Resource Management Plan Amendment for McGregor Range,* Las Cruces District Office, Bureau of Land Management, September 1990.

[53]An informal BLM publication titled "Military Use of Public Lands," dated January 1990, describes "several attempts" by the Army to "temporarily use over 1 million acres in the Las Cruces District which is outside the already existing White Sands Missile Range, Fort Bliss, Holloman AFB, and McGregor Range installations." More recently (January 23, 1995), Fort Bragg sent a memorandum to the BLM's Caballo Resource Area requesting "land maneuver rights" in support of "Exercise Roving Sands/Optic Cobra from 15 April to 9 May 1995." One BLM official volunteered that, although BLM would deny the request, the denial would be difficult to enforce as a result of lack of BLM personnel.

aries, while larger exercises can be increasingly conducted with simulations and twice-per-year visits to the National Training Center at Fort Irwin.[54] A similar argument is sometimes made for the Air Force, with verification of training realism to occur with occasional visits to the Red Flag exercises at Nellis range. Nevertheless, the nature of military operations changes at a much faster rate than DoD's ability to acquire new lands.

The examples highlighted on the left side of Figure 23 suggest that there may be opportunities for more intensive use of existing DoD lands. However, such cooperative efforts across DoD services has certainly not been the norm. Individuals at both Holloman Air Force Base and Fort Bragg unsuccessfully requested use of BLM land; but when a BLM district manager suggested to them that they utilize other local DoD land, they each complained of receiving low priority at other DoD bases. There is some multiservice planning, as evidenced by Holloman's use of a bombing range at Fort Bliss, and by the Air National Guard's Airspace Management Branch and regional airspace committees. Nonetheless, we are aware of few efforts to optimize multiservice land use on a regional level. The issue may have particular saliency in New Mexico because of the size of the facilities and their dependence on seeking tenants for tests, even if those tenants come from abroad. The DoD land resource in that area is so enormous that a multiservice review and optimization would seem warranted.

---

[54]General Accounting Office, *Army Training: Various Factors Create Uncertainty About Need for More Land,* GAO/NSIAD-91-103, April 1991.

New Initiatives Trigger Environmental Review and Ignite the Political Process

- Idaho acquisition resisted fiercely
- Success brings detailed legislative guidance
- Airspace initiatives scrutinized
- Opposition from "strange bedfellows"
  - Native Americans, environmentalists, ranchers, hunters, pilots, etc.
  - Native American/environmentalist synergy
  - anti-military
  - anti-federal

RAND *MR715-24*

Figure 24

Figure 23 highlighted a growing need for DoD to consider the use of extended lands for military operations. Figure 24 outlines implications of expanding military land use in terms of increased political attention focused on DoD natural and cultural resource programs. The above figure suggests that DoD needs to scrutinize its requests for new land and airspace and exhaust all multiservice options before making requests for use of additional land.

THE POLITICAL PROCESS FOR EXTENDED LANDS: PUBLIC INVOLVEMENT

Idaho and "Strange Bedfellows"

Unlike the almost purely regulatory-driven process that governs resource management within DoD bases, initiatives that cross base boundaries invite controversy and scrutiny. The trigger for this scrutiny is the requirement for formal environmental review under NEPA. Although NEPA does not imply substantive environmental responsibilities, it mandates public participation in decisionmaking and can serve as a rallying point for political opposition. NEPA can be used by opponents of DoD initiatives even when reasons for opposition have little to do with environmental concerns. The recent abandonment of Air Force plans for the Idaho Training Range (ITR) was the immediate result of a court decision related to NEPA.

The proposal for creation of ITR involves a long, complicated history that may well warrant a separate comprehensive "lessons-learned" analysis. The Air Force had proposed establishing training ranges in the southwest corner of Idaho to train crews stationed at Mountain Home Air Force Base. Most important was the composite wing, which is composed of diverse aircraft, that had been formed as a result of a realignment from George Air Force Base.

Several factors contributed to the ITR failure. Some personnel we interviewed argued that the Air Force took an "all-or-nothing" stance in presenting its completed expansion proposals. The base Public Information Office was inexperienced, and the Air Force was unable to clearly and convincingly demonstrate its training needs.[55] Opponents of the initiative argued that the state governor and the Air Force appeared to be bypassing the Engle Act, which requires an act of Congress for any military land acquisition over 5,000 acres.[56] Ultimately, it was the Air Force's failure to link realignment and land expansion that led a court to order a new environmental impact statement. The court also ordered the Air Force and the Greater Owyhee Legal Defense (GOLD) to reach agreement on an injunction regarding the operations of the composite wing at Mountain Home.[57] The order reflects the extent to which private groups can access the political process through NEPA and gain a role in federal decisionmaking. The Air Force has since decided not to abandon ITR even though a new Idaho initiative, nicknamed "Son of ITR," has been discussed and could face further public opposition.[58]

---

[55]No adequate rationale was given for, first, the original proposal to acquire 1.5 million acres of land and, then, the reduction of requirements to 24,000 acres.

[56]The Air Force has maintained that the arrangement did not violate the Engle Act. See USAF White Paper, *The Idaho Training Range*, Secretary of the Air Force, Office of Public Affairs, September 1994, p. 8.

[57] *The Idaho Statesman*, May 10, 1995.

[58]For one of many accounts in the press, see *Defense Environment Alert*, May 31, 1995, p. 22.

Even more significant, the experience illustrated that despite strong support from the state's governor, diverse local grassroots groups can coalesce in opposition to DoD initiatives on public lands and recruit influential supporters. Groups like the Sierra Club, the Wilderness Society, the Aircraft Owners and Pilots Association, the Shoshone Information Network, the Boise Peace Quilt Project, the Idaho Outfitters and Guides Association, the Idaho Sportsman's Coalition, the Idaho Sporting Congress, and numerous other diverse groups united under the banner of the Owyhee Canyonlands Coalition to oppose the Air Force initiative. The groups made the Air Force mission's impact on natural and cultural resources a public issue by publishing a full page ad in the western edition of *The New York Times* with the lead, "U.S. Bombers Strike Idaho" (Sept. 30, 1994). It also appears that the coalition had strong connections with at least one highly influential individual with direct access to the White House.

As noted in Figure 24, political opposition to DoD initiatives can lead to an alliance of "strange bedfellows" that will oppose DoD land-use initiatives. It is not only environmentalists, but a wide range of groups, some with a strong utilitarian focus on land use, that will join forces. Some of these groups are conservative politically and have traditionally been strong supporters of the military. Others may use their agenda to oppose DoD land-use initiatives because of their opposition to military activities of any kind.[59] Still others are motivated by the growing general skepticism toward the federal government.

A Special Constituency

One special category of groups that may occasionally oppose DoD initiatives is Native Americans. The widely perceived moral authority of Native American claims is proving to be politically potent, especially when combined with the organizational capabilities of environmental groups or other entities who may have a far less com-

---

[59]One BLM district manager noted that the recent public opposition to a 4,000-acre land withdrawal adjacent to Nellis AFB was not motivated by any obvious competing land use and speculated it may have been aroused by opposition to DoD activities in general.

pelling claim to the land but are better funded and have a longer tradition of political advocacy and organization.

Although there seems to be no new societal willingness to tackle the economic problems of Native American life, Native Americans have dramatically increased their effectiveness at utilizing the political process to pursue claims related to land use. Starting in the mid-1960s, Native Americans began to represent their own political concerns rather than relying on white "friends of the Indian" to do so. This strategy was supported by an emerging societal recognition of the tragic U.S. government role in the history of Native Americans. The timing of the shift also allowed Native Americans to benefit from the political lessons of other social movements.

The growth of this political skill was acknowledged on April 29, 1994, when the president, vice president, and every member of the president's cabinet (excluding Secretary Christopher) met with the leaders of more than 300 federally recognized tribes on the White House lawn.

The development of an effective strategy to meet the concerns of Native Americans has been addressed in a separate, companion report.[60] However, what is of particular note here is the synergy mentioned above. The Shoshone Tribe never formally joined the Owyhee Canyonlands Coalition, but the coalition made extensive use of the potential damage to Native American archaeological sites to oppose the expansion. In the previously mentioned *New York Times* advertisement, "sacred sites, graves and vision quest sites of the Paiute-Shoshone from nearby Duck Valley Reservation . . ." were among the most prominently listed resources "at risk." A similar informal alliance has also developed in Alaska in response to Air Force plans to expand airspace. As noted in the *Anchorage Daily News,* "The Air Force has given trappers, pilots, hunters, Natives and environmentalists something they agree on."

Finally, we should note that the largely separate political processes regarding federal lands and national security illustrated in Figure 6 have some important connections with Native American concerns.

---

[60]D. Mitchell and D. Rubenson, *Native American Affairs and the Department of Defense,* Santa Monica, Calif.: RAND, MR-630-OSD, 1996.

Senators McCain, Stevens, and Inouye have been deeply involved in both national security affairs and the concerns of Native American groups. The dual interest is not a coincidence (Alaska, Hawaii, and Arizona all have extensive tribal and DoD lands). It speaks to the need for DoD to carefully develop a strategy for addressing the concerns of Native Americans when it contemplates new uses of public lands, as well as when it operates existing bases.

THE POLITICAL PROCESS FOR EXTENDED LANDS: DETAILED LEGISLATION

Even when successful, new initiatives are governed by a different level of congressional oversight from that for existing bases. Although DoD is governed by minimal agency-specific legislative guidance, this pertains only to existing bases. In 1958, Congress passed the Engle Act, which mandated congressional approval for any withdrawal of public lands of more than 5,000 acres. This was the beginning of a change in the way in which DoD land expansions and exchanges would be governed. The requirement for congressional involvement creates the possibility for more-specific legislative guidance as to how withdrawn lands will be managed.

The potential for congressional engagement in management of new DoD lands occurred as early as 1982 with the law authorizing the acquisition of Piñon Canyon as a subinstallation of Fort Carson. Although much of Piñon was not withdrawn public land, Congress specified that the acquired land would be managed by utilizing the land rotation cycles specified in the environmental impact statement (EIS). The law authorizing the 1991 55,000-acre expansion of the Yakima Firing Range specified the need for additional environmental studies and that none of this land could be used for firing ranges. As will be discussed later, lands withdrawn in 1986 must adhere to several congressionally mandated instructions. Finally, the 1994 Desert Protection Act extended the withdrawal of China Lake but called upon the DoI and the Secretary of the Navy to develop joint management plans for protection of wildlife, recreation, grazing, and geothermal resources.

In summary, the relatively free hand that DoD is given to manage natural resources within its own bases can be significantly restricted whenever there is a change of boundaries. The nature of the restrictions imposed is generally a product of a complicated political process that does not occur for natural resource management within DoD bases.[61]

---

[61]We should note that the recent EIS for restationing the 3rd armored division at Fort Lewis—which did not involve any change in boundaries—contained a provision for implementing Integrated Training Area Management as a mitigation measure. Thus, the conclusion stated above can at least partially apply to conditions within base boundaries when the NEPA process is required.

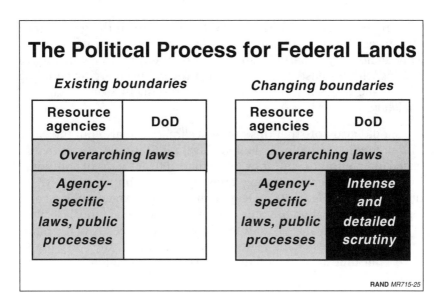

Figure 25

Utilizing the schematic shown in Figure 7, Figure 25 indicates that the governance process for DoD's management of federal lands varies depending on whether the issues involve existing boundaries or changing boundaries. In the latter case, DoD is subject to the same, if not more intense, political scrutiny as the large land management agencies. However, unlike the land management agencies, the structure and organization of the DoD natural and cultural resources program are not generally prepared to cope with such scrutiny.

Figure 25 also brings out an important point in regard to the individual military services. The natural and cultural resource management programs in the services have evolved from the problems they encounter at existing bases. With an airborne mission, the Air Force generally does not need to cope with the complex mission-ecology-law interaction faced by bases with intensive and expanding on-ground training. As such, its program is less prepared to deal with contentious and difficult management issues than that of the Army. However, it is the Air Force that has the most demanding requirements for changing boundaries when new technologies, tactics, or realignments occur. Thus, the level of contrast in the governance structures shown in Figure 25 is most dramatic for the Air Force. This dichotomy is partially mitigated by the Air Force's history of dealing with off-base noise issues. However, the emerging coupling of airspace issues to the NEPA process presents new organizational challenges.

We should also note that this political climate can also put the Navy into unfamiliar situations. Fallon Naval Air Station is currently engaged in an effort to withdraw more than 100,000 acres of additional BLM lands and renew existing lands under the Military Lands Withdrawal Act (see Figure 27). Despite these very charged political and legal processes, Fallon has only one lawyer stationed at the base, who is responsible for all legal matters. Given the complexity of the natural resource issues facing Fallon, it is surprising for the Navy not to have a full-time legal natural resource specialist at Fallon.

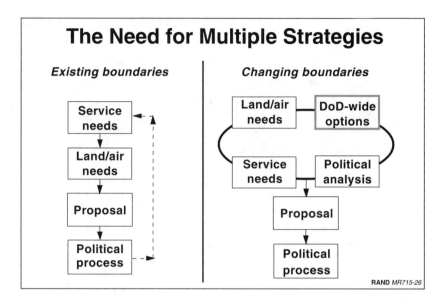

Figure 26

As mentioned earlier, the focal point for political opposition to DoD initiatives is formal public environmental review triggered under NEPA. Figure 26 illustrates two approaches to NEPA, depending on whether a particular NEPA case involves existing or changing DoD boundaries.

The left side of Figure 26 illustrates a process that has proved successful when applied to existing DoD lands. Military needs are translated into land and airspace needs and a formal proposal is generated with the emphasis on using land or air within a base's own boundaries or within its existing airspace. In these cases, there is normally little public interest and the initiative proceeds fairly smoothly.

Employing this same process to change boundaries of military land use introduces the feedback loop on the right side of Figure 26. Iteration now may proceed in the public political arena under NEPA requirements, and the requesting service must respond to public concerns regarding the boundary-changing initiative. This occurred at the Idaho Training Range, where Air Force proposals were ultimately abandoned in a highly visible and intensely contentious process.

Regarding present proposals for Rocky Mountain West, the approach illustrated on the right side of Figure 26 is probably more consistent with DoD needs when use of new land or airspace is contemplated. Rather than develop formal proposals quickly, the services should undertake a far more extensive, iterative process in which military needs regionally and across bases are explicitly analyzed in terms of their requirements for land and airspace. Those needs with minimal military value and maximal resource requirements could be dropped. More significant, the political environment now seems to mandate that the services exhaust options across all services before requesting new land and airspace. The absence of a carefully defined needs analysis has been utilized as an effective weapon by opponents of DoD initiatives.[62]

The need to examine all regional DoD-wide options for new initiatives involving a single service was clearly illustrated in the Arizona Air National Guard's ongoing efforts to acquire a new gunnery range and airspace for the Western Army National Guard (ANG) Training Center. After a decade of examining new land and airspace options, and being subject to the intense political process described on the right side of Figure 25, the Arizona ANG's current proposal is to utilize the resources at the Air Force's Goldwater range, where it appears that all ANG training objectives can be achieved.

We note that early political analysis in Figure 26 is not the same as early public involvement. The public has well-specified rights under NEPA that the services must acknowledge, respect, and facilitate. Nevertheless, agencies also have an obligation to ensure that their proposals, which in the case of DoD have a strong national rather than local interest, are carefully and intelligently prepared, taking full account of their feasibility in the local political arena. This is not to say, however, that proposals be presented to the public as complete and unalterable. Clear justification for new land and airspace needs

---

[62]In the previously referenced *New York Times* advertisement, the Owyhee Canyonlands Coalition stated, "The U.S. Air Force has failed to issue a promised assessment of its national training needs because such a report would show the proposed bombing range is unnecessary."

must be presented along with options to be discussed with the public.

A potentially critical point not illustrated in Figure 26 is appropriate use of outside contractors in the EIS process. One senior Air Force policymaker argued that overreliance on private contractors damaged the Air Force in Idaho. The environmental coordinator at Fort Lewis made a similar comment when comparing the NEPA process undertaken for the Yakima expansion with the restationing the 3rd armored division at Fort Lewis. While these stories are anecdotal, they are supported by more-systematic analyses of a failure to properly internalize the overall environmental program.[63]

We should note that as a result of the Idaho Training Range experience, the Air Force has created an office at headquarters (AF/X00A), attached to the operations function, that is charged with conducting iterative processes like that described above as well as for ensuring a level of connectivity between installations and headquarters that is not a by-product of the structure shown in Figure 9. A ranges and airspace office has also been established at the Air Combat Command. These offices have not yet resolved their long-term relationship with the installations or developed a tradition for engaging in new initiatives, and they do not have the charter to examine multiservice options fully. They may also be dependent on one or two key military officers with a special skill and inclination for this multidisciplinary task. Nonetheless, their creation is a positive step that needs to be reinforced and expanded into a fully capable multiservice office for natural and cultural resource policy planning.

One additional issue that must be considered in the context of a national needs assessment (both military land and airspace needs) is the role of the states and the National Guard. The guards are state agencies that, under normal circumstances, are under the authority of the individual governors. One of the controversies surrounding the Idaho Training Range involved applicability of the Engle Act, which requires congressional approval for withdrawals of over 5,000 acres. The issue was the act's applicability if active units use lands made available by a land exchange between BLM and the state. The

---

[63]See R-4220-A, 1992, pp. 16–18, and MR-453-A, pp. 63–64.

Air National Guard has proposed a number of expansion initiatives around the country. Although these are separate initiatives issued by individual state agencies, they are not perceived as such by many observers who are calling for a national needs assessment. The individual National Guard initiatives influence public and political sentiment regarding overall Air Force expansion initiatives. While those in DoD can separate initiatives by service and command, the public thinks "*DoD-wide*" in the broadest possible context.

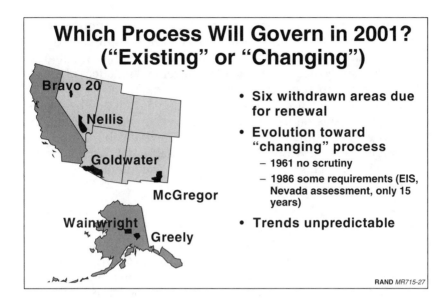

Figure 27

Figure 27 introduces a major issue that may defy the easy, "existing versus changing boundaries" categorization presented in Figure 26. As noted in Figure 4, 16 million of DoD's 25 million acres are withdrawn public lands. Seven million of these withdrawn acres must be renewed in the year 2001 by an act of Congress.[64] The six bases comprising this land are illustrated on the map in Figure 27.

While renewal will not require a change in boundaries, there are indications that the process may resemble that discussed as "changing boundaries" on the previous pages. While the original renewals in 1961 were approved with little scrutiny, the 1986 process reflected the new politics of the West. Rather than a 25 year renewal, Congress granted only 15 years, mandated an EIS prior to renewal in 2001, and required a health and ecological risk assessment of military activities in Nevada. Congress also became more specific about the BLM role

---

[64]Under FLPMA, BLM can extend segregation of withdrawn land if an application to extend the withdrawal was submitted but not acted on by Congress within two years following termination of the withdrawal and submission of the application.

in managing natural resources on the bases. In addition, Senator Metzenbaum (D-Ohio) raised questions about the rationale for the McGregor Range withdrawal. Shortly after the withdrawal, Congress mandated a study to review the land management practices of the six bases involved in the withdrawal.[65]   At the time, it was even suggested that the entire resource management function be turned over to BLM. Constraints on BLM budget and manpower ultimately led to the realization that such a transfer would be difficult to implement. Less obvious, but more fundamental, would be the difficulty in managing the military-ecology-legal interaction if those lands were not managed by DoD.

At present, the politics of process that will govern the renewals is unclear. The competition for federal lands and strong anti-federal feeling in the western states seem to imply a difficult (from DoD's perspective) political process. Even if DoD retains the lands, Congress could specify more detailed restrictions on how they are to be used. However, we should also note that these lands tend to be among the most remote and least competed-for lands in the West. There have been controversies at McGregor and Nellis but no strong coalitions have developed to oppose the renewals. Much of the public is unaware of the withdrawal process and has come to view these lands as permanent military areas.

Obviously, DoD will need to approach the process with great deliberation. One senior BLM official experienced with withdrawn military lands suggested that if DoD employs the processes suggested above for changing boundaries, then it is likely that less intensive legislated management would follow. He cautioned, however, that attempts to treat the issue as an internal matter (as has been done for "existing boundaries") could result in more public opposition and congressional scrutiny. These six renewals may be a prime opportunity for DoD to develop a program that comprehends internal issues but also is able to respond to vastly different external conditions when they become important.

Finally, we should note that the Air Force appears to have internalized many of the lessons of the Idaho Training Range and is moving

---

[65]General Accounting Office, *Defense and Interior Can Better Manage Land Withdrawn for Military Use*, GAO/NSIAP-94-87, April 1994.

forward with the EIS process in a manner similar to that recommended in this report. Credit must be given to the new offices at headquarters and the Air Combat Command for providing a significant level of command attention. In the authors' judgment, the Army and the Navy have not yet recognized the criticality of this issue, and there is a need to present a coordinated and consistent package to Congress.

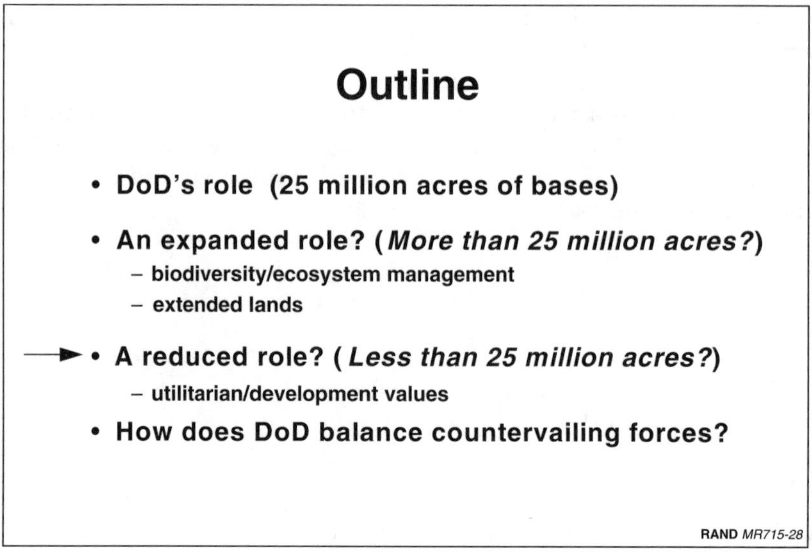

Figure 28

In the following pages, we will review some of the issues raised by the 104th Congress and their relevance to the preceding analysis.

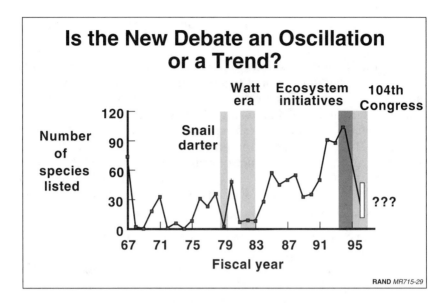

Figure 29

A major uncertainty is the fundamental review of environmental policy being undertaken by the 104th Congress. Figure 29 uses one indicator of shifts in federal politics' influence on environmental policy—annual listings of threatened and endangered species—to pose the question of the long-term implications of this review.

Figure 29 shows that the number of new listings under the Endangered Species Act has oscillated with political events. The famous controversy over the snail darter—which threatened to prevent the completion of the Telico Dam—led to a temporary halt on listings in late 1970s. New listings virtually ceased during the early Reagan administration when then Secretary of the Interior James Watt implemented a strong utilitarian focus to DoI policy. However, the reaction to Watt, and the ability of key groups to use the courts to force listings, has led to a steady increase in the number of annual listings since 1984. Annual listings peaked in FY 1994, and in response to the congressional elections of 1994, the U.S. Fish and Wildlife Service imposed a moratorium on further listings in April 1995. However, listings between the election and that date, as well as a backlog of court-ordered listings, made fiscal year 1995 an active listing year. With the self-imposed moratorium continuing, we expect few listings in FY 1996.

Even though Figure 29 points to environmental policy as inherently oscillatory, it should be noted that measures related to enforcement, such as listings, budget allocations, or executive policy are more susceptible to oscillations than changes in law. It has proven to be relatively easy to turn some environmental policies "on" and "off" in this context. In contrast, environmental laws have proved difficult to reauthorize, and the emergence of coalitions strong enough to make fundamental legislative revisions appears to be a far less frequent event than congressional budget alteration that leads to changes in enforcement practices.

The debate in the 104th Congress represents, at a minimum, the type of oscillation shown in Figure 29. Congress can surely reduce budgets for enforcement and induce short-term changes in environmental policy. Some short-term changes can produce unintended but lasting ecological effects. They may also result in unintended institutional effects that are difficult to reverse. The early Reagan administration's go-slow approach to hazardous waste cleanup led to significantly more stringent and demanding hazardous waste laws in 1984 and 1986. However, we should note that, along with such short-term levers as enforcement budget cuts, Congress is approaching environmental policy changes by fundamentally reviewing the underlying statutes. If there are sweeping changes in these laws, then the election of 1994 could be viewed as the start of a new trend in environmental policy. However, the extent to which the current review represents such an event, as opposed to an oscillation, may take several years to determine. At a minimum, it will be necessary to monitor the outcome of the 1996 election before making even a tentative judgment.

What We Know

- **25 years of serial public opinion surveys:**
  - **– nonutilitarian trend**
  - **– segmented views**

- **Flexibility is current focus:**
  - **– cost/benefit analysis**
  - **– expanded national security exemption?**

- **State programs grew in early eighties**

- **No serious debate about formal environmental review**

RAND *MR715-30*

Figure 30

With insufficient information or perspective to forecast the implications of the 104th Congress, Figure 30 summarizes some of the factors DoD should consider in evaluating the new political signals.

We note that a wide body of public opinion surveys indicate a slowly growing trend in the American population that places greater value on the aesthetic and nonutilitarian uses of natural resources.[66] This perspective is supported by 25 years of serial opinion polling. The demographics of the existing value structure, combined with demographic projections of the American population, are evidence that the trend will continue. We must note that there are few data in several demographic categories, such as the ways in which the rapidly growing Hispanic population views natural resources.

---

[66]These data and a complete bibliography have been documented in an as-yet-unpublished report prepared for RAND by S. Kellert on trends in attitudes toward natural resource and wildlife and the implications for the U.S. Department of Defense. The report provides a review and synthesis of a wide range of publicly available literature and data compiled by Dr. Kellert and others tracking public attitudes toward wildlife over several decades.

Although the referenced surveys have proved to be consistent and objectively administered, there are methodological issues as well as basic limitations in the utility of opinion surveys. Ultimately, predictions using demographic projections must be considered cautiously.

These same opinion surveys also indicate that, despite the long-run trend, oscillations in the political process are likely to continue. Values in American society are highly segmented. Utilitarian and development values remain strong and influential even if there is a broad level of support for nonutilitarian perspectives. Convincing evidence was felt during the early stages of the Clinton presidency when the administration sought to raise grazing fees on federal land. Even though ranching interests account for a significantly smaller part of the population and economic output in western states than in past decades, those interests were extremely well organized and able to deflect President Clinton's efforts. Certainly the election of the 104th Congress demonstrates that, even if a broad nonutilitarian-value trend exists, it is not necessarily a decisive factor in individual elections.

This suggests that oscillations should be expected in the political process governing federal lands. It also suggests that wildlife values are a fundamental core value in American society despite sharply different and contradictory perspectives. As the DoD seeks to build an enduring program, it will need to prepare for increasingly diverse and oscillatory pressures and guidance.

We also know that the current congressional review of the overarching laws pertaining to total ecosystem management is oriented toward providing flexibility and discretion in balancing economic and ecological concerns. One of the most frequently discussed means of incorporating flexibility is to build cost/benefit tests into the law. The meaning of this in a military context has not been discussed in any detail. In fact, congressional focus in its debate over environmental legislation is clearly on private-sector interests and the large federal land management agencies, as it has always been. There has been some explicit recognition of DoD in these debates, but it does not appear that any significant changes will be made in environmental law specific to DoD. For example, a Senate Environment Panel Hearing was held on the impact of the Endangered Species Act at

Fort Bragg.[67] Senator Lauch Faircloth (R-North Carolina) followed the hearing with the suggestion that base commanders be given the discretion to invoke exemptions to the act. At this time, Senator Faircloth's language appears to have been dropped from legislation likely to pass in the near future. We should, however, note that the Secretary of Defense already has the authority to make exemptions but has never chosen to do so.

The 104th Congress does not seem to have placed significant priority on reevaluating NEPA and the process of formal and public environmental review of new federal actions. Although NEPA is almost entirely a formality for activities that take place within existing base boundaries, the lack of debate about NEPA suggests it will remain a mechanism around which diverse groups rally to oppose federal initiatives.

Now that more than full year has passed since the 1994 elections, we also know that any fundamental changes in environmental statutes will come slowly and with great deliberation. Although Congress is anxious to conduct a fundamental review, it has not yet significantly altered any major pieces of environmental legislation. At the time of this report, new versions of the Endangered Species Act have been written, but they are likely to be extensively debated and modified many times before they are eventually approved. The House recently voted not to press forward with 17 specific changes in environmental legislation that had seemed to be a major priority of the new Congress just one year ago.[68]

It is also important to note that state environmental programs grew in response to lax federal enforcement of environmental laws in the early 1980s. Obviously, we cannot be sure that the states would re-

---

[67]Friday, March 17, 1995, panel hearing before the Senate Committee on Environment and Public Works. The panel included George Frampton, Assistant Secretary for Fish and Wildlife and Parks, Department of Interior; General C. Stiner (Ret.) former commander of Fort Bragg; L. D. Walker, Deputy Assistant Secretary of the Army; and Major General Richard E. Davis, Deputy Commanding General for XVIII Airborne Corps and Fort Bragg.

[68]The House vote took place on November 2, 1995.

spond in a similar manner in the 1990s; however, we are reminded of the diverse centers of power and authority that govern environmental affairs.

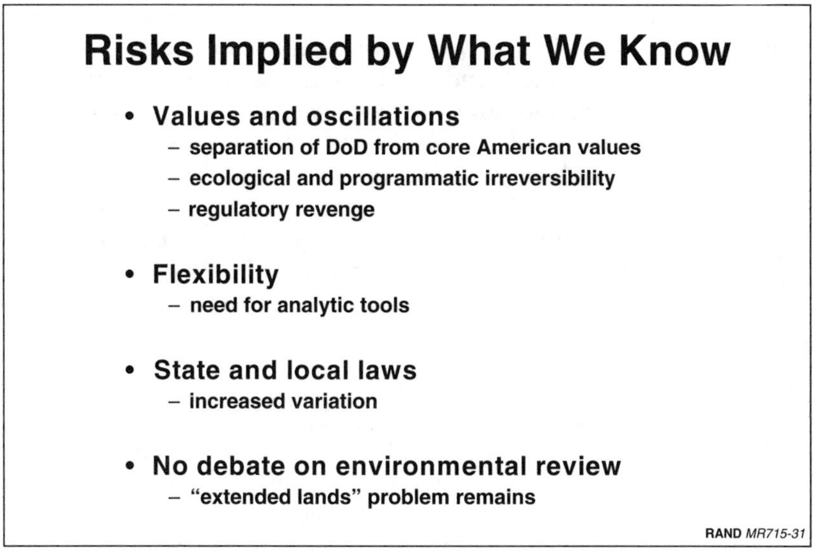

Risks Implied by What We Know

- **Values and oscillations**
  - separation of DoD from core American values
  - ecological and programmatic irreversibility
  - regulatory revenge

- **Flexibility**
  - need for analytic tools

- **State and local laws**
  - increased variation

- **No debate on environmental review**
  - "extended lands" problem remains

RAND *MR715-31*

Figure 31

At this point, many key environmental laws, such as the ESA, and ex-ecutive branch policy diverge in some important ways from the pri-orities and values expressed by many members of the 104th Congress. While DoD is subject to direct command from the execu-tive branch, DoD nonetheless retains significant discretion in build-ing and designing an internal natural and cultural resource program. The executive branch has also sent significantly less-ambitious environmental signals since the 1994 elections. Some in DoD may view the congressional debate as the emergence of a new trend and may be anxious to realize cost savings by reducing the size of the program. While savings would not be large, these factions would ar-gue that there would be accompanying benefits in terms of reducing the need for command attention and that the organizational linkages and multidisciplinary skills that have developed would no longer need to be maintained. Figure 31 highlights some possible risks in making these assumptions and highlights new challenges implied by the current debate.

One risk is that a rapid downsizing of the natural and cultural re-sources program could separate DoD from what may be a core

American value. Although DoD's mission is military training and readiness, there is a broad-based assumption that, in the long run, the ability to be trained and ready requires a close connection between the military and American society. Exemptions to American law, policy, and cultural standards are granted only occasionally, with great care and deliberation, and normally when there is a convincing and direct effect on the ability to be trained and ready. While the United States could pursue an aggressive program of ecological protection without DoD lands (and despite their significance), the key issue is the extent to which DoD needs to share in such a vision.

Of a less philosophical nature, downsizing the program puts at risk DoD's investment in building internal capability and relationships. If current political events prove to be no more than a significant oscillation, DoD will not want to find itself having to relearn the lessons of the past decade. In such a future situation, DoD may find itself challenged to cope with regulators buoyed by a return of regulatory priorities and angry at the abandonment of carefully negotiated conservation plans. A similar estimate can be said to characterize the implementation of hazardous waste policy in the late 1980s.

Oddly enough, the direction of congressional review of the overarching laws, with its emphasis on flexibility, carries challenges and also highlights weaknesses in DoD's natural and cultural resource program. DoD has never invoked the National Security exemption for ESA partly because it has not had convincing information on military impacts. A new exemption procedure might contain less-demanding criteria, but DoD remains far from being able to explain military impacts of environmental law at virtually any level. If a cost/benefit formulation ultimately characterizes the law, DoD will need to develop unique methodologies that translate military measures into economic ones. In general, greater flexibility implies the need for greater knowledge of environmental impacts and an increased ability to defend decisions.

Similarly, reduction in the intensity of federal laws could be followed by increased diversity and scrutiny of state and local enforcement on DoD lands. Such diversity already exists for many hazardous waste issues and has proved to be a vexing problem in evaluating the validity of requests from installations for environmental funding.

Finally, we note that the absence of a significant debate on NEPA suggests that many of the issues related to competition for land in the West will be unaffected by the current congressional review. As previously noted, many of the groups competing for resources are politically conservative and hold strong utilitarian views toward natural resources. In many ways, the issues in the West are not environmental issues but issues of land-use planning. NEPA is merely a process that forces these issues into the public forum.

To summarize, the implications of the discussion in the 104th Congress are potentially far-reaching but may be uncertain for several years. If the debate proves to be another oscillation in the political process, then DoD may take significant risks by reacting strongly to current political signals in implementing environmental laws. If additional flexibility is the ultimate output of the debate, DoD may actually need to enhance its natural and cultural resource management capabilities to exercise this flexibility.

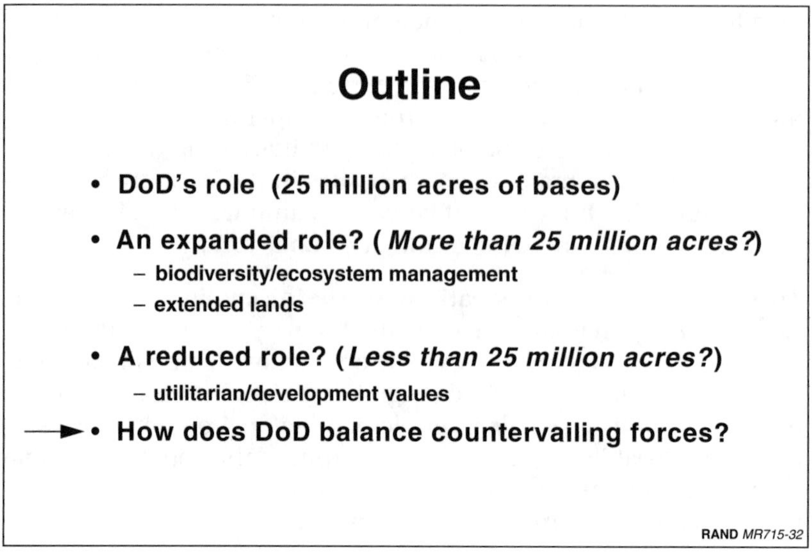

Figure 32

In the following pages, we summarize the preceding discussion and make a series of recommendations to help DoD build a more effective and responsive natural and cultural resource management program.

How Can the Program Be Broadened?

- **DoD faces "squeeze:"**
  - geographical scope of military mission
  - ecological islands
  - competition for federal land

- **Despite uncertainty, scope of program growing**
  - bases, regions, "extended lands"

- **Political governance different for each**

- **Bases still fundamental unit**

RAND *MR715-33*

Figure 33

A central conclusion of this report is highlighted in Figure 33: DoD's natural and cultural resource program requires greater breadth, particularly in the areas of planning and strategic analysis. The overriding reason is the "squeeze" between the growing geographical expanse of military requirements and the intensity of land use in regions around military bases and in "extended lands." While ecosystem management to preserve biodiversity has been identified as the primary reason for considering a broader role, it is actually core DoD interests of legal compliance and mission preservation, which only partially overlap with biodiversity concerns, that provide this motivation.

A major challenge is to build programs at the bases that can selectively respond to all three types of challenges: bases, regions, and extended lands—each of which is governed by different political conditions. The fragmented structure of DoD's land holdings implies that the base-level program will remain the fundamental unit of management.

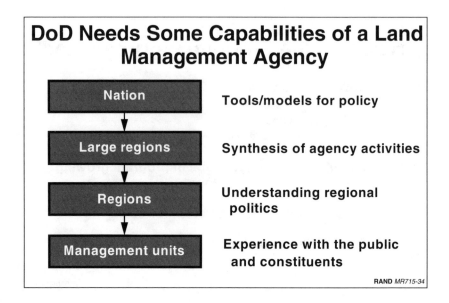

Figure 34

Stated somewhat differently, DoD needs some of the capabilities of an idealized land management agency. This agency may at times require a strong outward orientation, the ability to synthesize and plan for resource use at a regional level, and an understanding of local political processes in order to determine the appropriate level of engagement in regional habitat planning; and it may increasingly need the capability to explain its problems and impacts in terms of costs and benefits.

Land management agencies are organized on a geographical basis, thereby facilitating (in theory) the development of the tools, models, and political perspectives appropriate for each level of aggregation. Equally importantly is a tradition and culture that is responsive to outside constituencies.

For obvious reasons, DoD is not organized like a land management agency. Nonetheless, it requires some of the perspectives that flow from such an organizational design. The following figures present two sequential steps that might allow DoD to adopt some of those features.

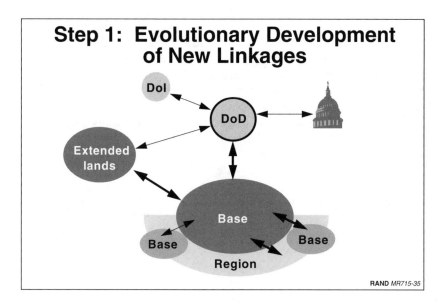

Figure 35

Figure 35 highlights evolutionary steps DoD can take to build the perspective described on the preceding page. It involves augmentation of the capabilities at existing bases. In particular, it focuses on building the capabilities at bases to cope with the challenge of on-base management, carefully calculated engagement in regional habitat planning, and preparation for the environmental review process on "extended lands." Bases would need to develop a better understanding of activities and resource use at nearby bases and of regional patterns in habitat conditions. Staffs at key bases would need to be supplemented to meet these requirements.

In this evolutionary structure, a multiservice policy planning staff at headquarters—with a tradition for direct coordination with bases—takes on a critical role. Air Force X00A is beginning to provide a single service blueprint for such an office. Since there is neither the resources nor the need for every base to have the full slate of capabilities for every situation, each base would develop the capabilities most applicable to the type of challenges it faces. Since the existing structure does not offer capability for regional planning and synthesis, there is a strong need for a centralized office. This central office would identify where these capabilities are lacking, oversee activities for extended lands, and monitor and supplement the on-base efforts to engage in off-base activities. It would by necessity be staffed by a mixture of civilian natural-resource professionals and uniformed members of each of the services. We also note that the multiservice planning team should create a liaison function with BLM, since that agency has a potentially important impact on a majority of DoD lands and DoD's access to extended lands.[69]

---

[69]We credit the suggestion for a liaison to BLM's Dwight Hempel, who tracks or is involved with processing military withdrawals; use of "extended lands," including overflight issues; and base closures, including terminating withdrawals.

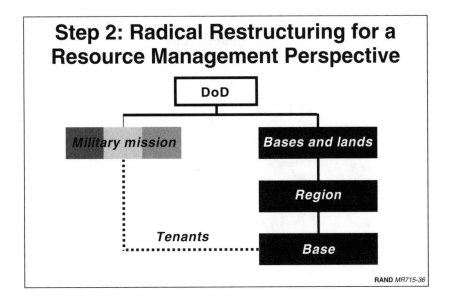

Figure 36

Figure 36 shows another option that involves radical restructuring of the chain of command to allow DoD to nearly replicate the structure of a land management agency. The structure is consistent with the analysis presented in this report, but its adoption would require consideration of other issues related to installation management and the importance of the unitary command structure. Consideration of this option should be delayed until after implementation of the steps highlighted in Figure 35.

In this option, bases and lands are separated from the military mission, and a new multiservice support command is established. It would be operated largely by civilians, but because of the intersection of many support operations with the military mission (such as natural and cultural resource management), it would be commanded by a small group of military officers with a career specialty in installation or resource management.

The advantages of this structure are obvious. It allows organization around geographic considerations and facilitates development of the appropriate perspectives at different levels of aggregation. Regional offices would be needed to fulfill the task of monitoring DoD resource use across the services for each region.

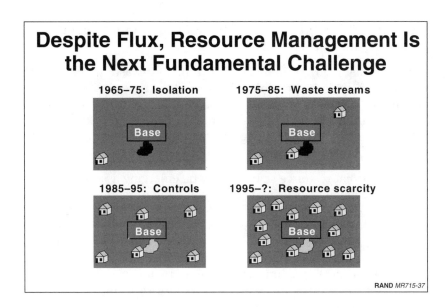

Figure 37

We close the briefing with a notional diagram that indicates that DoD's environmental challenge may be undergoing a fundamental shift.

As illustrated in Figure 37, DoD's environmental challenge has been driven by external trends, values, and forces. Prior to the mid 1970s, many DoD bases were isolated, and pollution from these bases (illustrated by the dark cloud adjacent to the base in the upper left of the figure) had few effects. By the late 1970s, suburban sprawl (the upper right of the figure) had led many communities to voice concerns about hazardous waste from DoD and Department of Energy (DoE) facilities, and Congress directed both DoD and DoE to develop a major environmental program.

The past 10 years have involved developing a response to the problem of wastes at defense facilities. While many cleanup challenges remain, and pollution prevention is only partially implemented, waste disposal is now carried out with legally correct procedures, and systems are in place to address unsolved problems. Many community fears have been addressed by both substantive actions and careful explanation of problems.

Thus, although DoD's financial obligations for waste management remain high, with the possible exception of the base closure process, which still suffers from fundamental problems, this management may not require as much attention from senior DoD policymakers as it has in the past. This "solving" of the problem is illustrated by the lightening of the cloud in the lower left of the figure.

We suggest that resource scarcity may be emerging as a new fundamental challenge. Because of continued habitat fragmentation outside of bases and competition for federal lands, it is increasingly difficult for DoD to access the land, air, and water needed to conduct military training. The financial costs of coping with this problem will be far less than those incurred for the problem of waste management. However, the solutions will be more vexing, have a greater impact on the military mission, and require continuous attention from senior military and civilian leadership. To cope with this challenge, DoD will need to expand the scope and sophistication of its natural and cultural resource management program and maintain institutional support for these efforts.

Chapter Two

CONCLUSIONS

Our central conclusion is that, despite significant uncertainty in the national environmental debate, the risks associated with downsizing the natural and cultural resource management program far outweigh the minimal savings that can be obtained. Even more significant, the breadth of DoD involvement is increasing, and corresponding capabilities are required. This expanded involvement is a result of two conflicting trends—the geographical expansion of military operations and population growth in regions where DoD has most of its lands. The current program should be enhanced with capabilities for planning and strategic analysis to cope with this "squeeze."

Returning to the introduction of the report where we discussed the conflicting political signals impinging on DoD's natural and cultural resource program, we answer the policy questions presented earlier in the following manner:

1. *What internal and external factors currently provide the motivation and political framework for DoD natural and cultural resource management?*

   The management of natural and cultural resources on DoD lands is not subject to intense public or congressional scrutiny. As such, DoD's current program is motivated by two goals: legal compliance and maintenance of the land for military training. DoD now recognizes that there can be a complex interaction between these two objectives and that there is a need for a broad and long-range interpretation of requirements. DoD has built an inward-looking program that focuses on this complex problem and has not yet needed the more outward-looking capabilities of the large land management agencies. We should also note that DoD leadership does at times choose to engage in additional conservation goals that enhance public support and ensure connectivity to societal values.

2. *What external trends may ultimately force DoD to develop a more outward-looking and broader orientation toward natural and cultural resource management?*

Competition for federal lands in the West, regional habitat degradation in the East and on the Pacific Coast, and new scientific principles imply that the core DoD interests of legal compliance and mission preservation will be increasingly affected by natural resource concerns beyond the boundaries of DoD lands. When addressing these issues, DoD will be subject to far more intense political scrutiny than it experiences within the boundaries of its bases. President Clinton's policy of ecosystem management provides a broad-based strategy for dealing with some of these issues. However, the policy must be applied with selectivity and adapted for the DoD's unique role as a federal land manager and for the current limitations of DoD's natural and cultural resource management program. To cope with the increased competition for federal lands in the west, DoD will need to gain a better understanding of its cross-service regional roles and uses of land and airspace.

3. *What external trends may allow DoD to reduce its emphasis on natural and cultural resource management and how enduring are these trends?*

The 1994 election may signal a significant shift in the nation's approach to natural resource management. However, there is strong popular identification with natural resource values, and the new Congress does not seem to be moving to drastically alter DoD's responsibilities. One outcome of this process may be to increase the span of DoD discretion with a corresponding greater need to develop analytical tools to support requests for flexibility.

4. *How does DoD integrate countervailing external signals into an effective natural resource management program that reflects so-*

cietal values and accounts for the need to maintain lands and waters for military training?

The risks associated with downsizing the natural and cultural resource management program far outweigh the minimal savings that can be obtained. More generally, DoD can best manage the significant uncertainties by expanding the strategic planning and analytical capabilities of the program.

In many ways the capabilities described in the answers to questions 2, 3, and 4 above are those of an idealized (in theory) resource management agency. Resource management agencies are organized in a manner that allows for regional synthesis of agency activities, awareness of local and regional political processes, the use of national planning tools, and a general outward-looking orientation. Although DoD cannot be organized like a resource management agency, it can strive to develop these capabilities.

DoD's challenge is to build these capabilities into the existing system located at bases. The current base-level program has developed in response to a relatively tame political process, in contrast to that required for broader engagement.

Programatically, we recommend at the base level

- stabilizing and augmenting natural resource staffs at bases. These staffs have never reached sufficient numbers to properly address on-base management issues and are generally unprepared to cope with complex political environments.

- unifying natural resource funding to allow more flexibility for strategic planning and analysis and eliminate the need to conduct revenue-generating activities such as timber harvesting, grazing, agriculture, etc.

- developing a decisionmaking system and funding mechanism to allow bases to invest in off-base concerns and mitigation strategies as appropriate.

- creating, on a pilot level, a new position at bases analogous to the base transition coordinator in base closure. This individual's job would be oriented toward those external issues that affect base natural resource management in the short or long run.

At a headquarters level, we recommend

- using the initial work from DoD's biodiversity dialogue, continued working toward development of a "military conservation biology" that incorporates the principles of this new science while accounting for near-term programmatic requirements and limitations. This can be initiated by using a critical DoD installation to conduct a "model" natural resource planning exercise that incorporates the principles of ecosystem management and conservation biology in a DoD framework. This would consist of analysis of the base's role in the regional ecology and a description of the active management processes needed to obtain conservation goals at the base. A comprehensive land-use plan that incorporated all human (including mission) activities at the base would be required. Explicit analysis of how such an approach differs from the current "compliance-oriented" approach should be made.

- in developing a strategy for the future of the program, explicitly including consideration of the institutional and organizational investment that has occurred in the last 10 years to build the current adequate, but fragile, natural and cultural resource program.

- prioritizing resource management actions by identifying where on DoD's 25 million acres a close interaction among law, ecology, and mission planning is required for successful land management and which lands serve as buffer zones or unusable terrain (from a military perspective) and thus require less intense management. In making this dichotomy, planners must remain sensitive to ecological processes that cross artificial boundaries.

- expanding on the new Air Force ranges and airspace planning office at headquarters by creating a multiservice policy planning office at headquarters to conduct the tasks highlighted in the preceding discussion of the "evolutionary option." Its first task should be to review the processes for renewing the six major bases under the Military Lands Withdrawal Act.

- conducting a review of all DoD uses, and applications for use, of extended lands as a second task for the policy planning staff. The review should include National Guard uses—which are linked in the public's mind to active-force initiatives—and should be combined with a military needs assessment. This should lead to a systematic ranking of both military priorities and resource needs. Requests of relatively minor military importance that imply significant resource needs should be scrutinized.

- reviewing DoD policy toward Native American groups in recognition of the unique role Native Americans play among the groups competing for access to "extended lands" in the West. More specific recommendations are provided in MR-630-OSD, 1996.

- assigning a liaison to work with BLM personnel monitoring the status of withdrawn land and to increase DoD institutional knowledge of the lands withdrawal process.

- conducting an Air Force–led "lessons-learned" analysis for the Idaho experience. (The Army's analysis of a natural resource management setback at Fort Bragg has proved to be invaluable.) The objective of such an analysis should be to determine systemic determinants of the problems rather than to focus on individual blame.

- exploring ways to promote organizational learning from the diverse NEPA processes conducted by DoD. This would at a minimum include a greater level of internal involvement in many EIS processes.

- expanding the current examination of life-cycle costs of new weapon systems, which has begun to consider costs of pollution and waste disposal, to incorporate land use and airspace needs.

Finally, we note that DoD's expanding involvement with natural and cultural resource management may represent a fundamental shift in the nature of its environmental responsibilities. While the decade between 1985 and 1995 was oriented toward the problems of hazardous wastes at DoD facilities, those problems have been largely solved in terms of the need for senior DoD policymakers to engage in and develop new policy approaches. An expanding population and a geographically expanding military mission imply that managing for resource scarcity is emerging as a new fundamental challenge. This challenge will require less financial investment than the problem of hazardous wastes, but it will require more time and attention of senior DoD management and will have a more direct impact on the military mission. *We conclude that DoD's role in resource management and the nation's stake in that role involve "More Than 25 Million Acres."*